LAURA ASHLEY

Decorating
with
PATTERNS & TEXTURES

LAURA ASHLEY

Decorating
w i t h
PATTERNS & TEXTURES

USING COLOR, PATTERN AND TEXTURE IN THE HOME

JANE STRUTHERS

STEP-BY-STEP TEXT BY ALISON WORMLEIGHTON
Special photography by David Brittain

CROWN TRADE PAPERBACKS
NEW YORK

Edited by Alison Wormleighton
Designed by Christine Wood
Special photography by David Brittain
Styling by Jacky Boase
Illustrations by Kate Simunek

First published in the United Kingdom in 1996 by Ebury Press
Random House, 20 Vauxhall Bridge Road, London SW1V 2SA

Published by Crown Trade Paperbacks, 201 East 50th Street,
New York, New York 10022. Member of the Crown Publishing Group.

Random House Inc. New York, Toronto, London, Sydney, Auckland

http://www.randomhouse.com/

CROWN TRADE PAPERBACKS and colophon are trademarks of Crown Publishers Inc.

Manufactured in Great Britain by Butler and Tanner Ltd, Frome, Somerset

Library of Congress Cataloguing-in-Publication Data is available on request

ISBN 0-517-88733-9

10 9 8 7 6 5 4 3 2 1

First American Edition

Contents

Introduction

The variety of patterns available in home furnishings today is more extensive than ever, and Laura Ashley offers a unique range of fabrics and wallpapers – from bold, painterly florals and delicately drawn sprigs to empire stripes and classic tartans. In the 1990s, texture has become as important as pattern, with home furnishing products also available in a wide diversity of textures, from rich jacquard weaves and rustic wicker chairs to glossy chintzes and smooth ceramics.

This book offers you a host of new decorating ideas to help you create beautiful rooms that not only incorporate successful combinations of patterns and textures but also have a sense of character and individuality entirely your own.

Eight original rooms show how combinations of different patterns and textures create a variety of decorating styles, be it a traditional living room, a rustic dining room, a contemporary bedroom, an informal kitchen in a vacation home, or an eclectic family room. Nature and the seasons have been the inspiration for many of the decorating schemes in the book, such as the family room based on warm autumnal colors and motifs; the bedroom decorated with an apple orchard theme; and the garden transformed into a magical place for a summer party.

As well as a multitude of inspiring ideas, more than thirty original step-by-step projects show you how to create the looks yourself. The projects range from quick ways to make striking cushions, tablecloths, and slipcovers to unusual curtains and tiebacks and even a stunning floral tent for a garden party. There are also projects to produce interesting textures and unusual effects with stenciling and stamping; painting ceramic tiles, enamelware, and terra-cotta; antiquing and distressing wood; gilding and decoupage. All of the projects and decorating ideas have that distinctive quality that makes them essentially Laura Ashley.

The delicate colors, soft textures, and complex patterns of these old roses are echoed in the print of the nearby bed linen. Like roses, floral fabrics are widely popular and very diverse.

CHAPTER ONE

Pattern and Texture

Nature is rich with an incredible wealth of patterns and textures. Nothing in nature is without pattern, from the shapes of green leaves on the branches of a tree against a blue sky to the pattern of white daisies in green grass or the concentric design of rose petals around a stem. The different textures in nature are also diverse, from the roughness of bark to the sparkle of grass glistening in the sunlight to the silky look of delphinium flowers.

Decorating schemes should also include a variety of different pattern and textures. Aside from color, the most important elements in decorating are pattern and texture. They should be considered for all the different aspects of decorating: for walls and floors, textiles, furniture, decorative accessories, collections, and even the smallest details such as the buttons on a pillow or a display of fresh flowers. It is your particular choice of patterns and textures as well as your collections of objects – a display of books or a collection of pitchers on a mantelpiece – that will give your room its unique personality.

Texture and pattern are, of course, virtually inseparable. For instance, pretty floral chintz fabrics not only have the pattern of the flowers and leaves printed on them but also the glazed texture of the cotton; a wooden table has the pattern of the grain of wood as well as an interesting texture.

The diamond-shaped raised texture of the linen fabric beautifully sets off the pattern of the faded florals on a dusky background. This traditional fabric is well suited to the classic lines of the Queen Anne chair.

INTRODUCING PATTERN

Although pattern comes into a scheme from virtually everything that is in the room, the most important patterns are in the wallpapers and curtains, upholstery and colorful rugs, because these cover the largest area.

There are innumerable patterned papers and fabrics to choose from. For walls, the most popular patterns are generally stripes, florals, and geometrics, as well as the new wallpapers that subtly imitate paint effects. Stripes may be particularly appropriate in more formal rooms, such as dining rooms or elegant living rooms, while simple florals are often used for informal living rooms, family rooms, and bedrooms.

Geometrics, such as checks or simple, evenly spaced fleurs-de-lys or Indian woodblock motifs, can be the perfect compromise between a plain painted wall and an elaborate, highly patterned wall covering. Geometrics introduce subtle texture to the room, revealing an interesting pattern when looked at closely.

The key to successful decorating is a subtle combination of different patterns. If you fall in love with a beautiful floral wallpaper for your bedroom, choose simple striped or plain curtains and perhaps a small check for a chair and the edging of a bedspread. Alternatively, choose a wonderful floral chintz for the curtains and a couple of pillows, then pick out one of the flower colors for a bold striped or paint-effect wallpaper.

Fabrics are sold in a wide variety of patterns, from traditional, formal designs such as chinoiserie and toile de Jouy to contemporary florals, ginghams, and stripes, as well as novelty prints, which are particularly suitable for children's bedrooms, kitchens, or bathrooms. It doesn't matter whether you choose just one or two patterned fabrics for a room or ten – so long as they all work together.

There are endless places to incorporate fabric in a room and all are crucial to making it comfortable and inviting. Use it to upholster chairs, sofas, footstools, and ottomans, or to cover accent pillows and floor pillows. Make it into curtains or draperies, valances, and shades; four-poster bed curtains and bed coverings; tablecloths and napkins.

If you have found some patchwork quilts, old bedspreads, or antique textiles, turn them into wall hangings or sofa throws. Introduce small areas of pattern in a room by using fabric for decorative details such as shelf edgings, rag rugs, and trimmings.

Patterns can be combined in several ways to create a successful decorative scheme. Some patterns go especially well together, such as ginghams and simple country florals, or traditional florals and stripes. The combination of one large pattern and one small one is also attractive, provided the larger pattern does not completely swamp the smaller one. Mix different patterns by using one for the curtains and another for the upholstery, or combine two patterns in one area, such as a window treatment in which a paisley print is used for the valance and a striped fabric for the curtains. The safest way to do this is for the two patterns to incorporate many of the same colors, which will then act as a unifying force.

You can use several different patterns together, but this will work best if you follow two basic guidelines. First, the patterns will probably look best if they are different scales. For example, do not combine two large, colorful, dominant florals – instead use a large floral design with a small, simply spaced one. Second, several different patterns will work well together if the fabrics all coordinate through a similar use of the same color or colors.

Combining patterns is made particularly easy by design companies such as Laura Ashley that produce fabric collections consisting of different patterns designed to go together.

INTRODUCING TEXTURE

Everything has a texture. It may be subtle or difficult to discern, such as a matte-painted wall, or it may be very obvious, such as the surface of an antique tapestry pillow.

Interior decorators divide texture into the categories of hard and soft – hard textures include wood, flooring, walls, and furniture while soft textures include textiles and carpets. The key to a successful room is combining the hard and soft textures so that they complement each other.

It is important to strike a harmonious balance

The crisp lines of colorwash stripe wallpaper next to a translucent muslin with a pattern of delicately drawn botanical florals demonstrate how successfully a contemporary stripe can be combined with a traditional floral.

– rooms that are full of hard textures may seem uncomfortable, inhospitable places while rooms that go to the other extreme and consist mostly of soft textures may seem claustrophobic or suffocating. In most rooms, it is easy to find a good overall balance of hard and soft textures, but you may wish to experiment with small details. Try to combine hard and soft textures in surprising, innovative ways, such as hanging a linen curtain from a rustic, black iron curtain rod, putting a kilim on a wooden floor, or piling a colorful collection of tapestry and velvet pillows on a wooden settle.

Before you decorate a room, it is important to examine the existing areas of interesting texture. There may be more of these than you realize at first. For instance, the ceiling may be plain or it may be decorated with beautiful plaster relief-work; perhaps it is surrounded by a lovely plaster frieze or covered in wood paneling. You may have wooden beams running across your ceiling, an attractive tiled floor, or old wooden lintels at the top of the window frames. The walls may be rough-textured or perhaps paneled. Or you might have a pair of beautiful mahogany side tables or an ethnic Indian coffee table which you want to make into focal points of the room. These are all areas of texture that can be highlighted in your decorative scheme.

Once you have surveyed the room, you can decide which areas would look good with extra texture. For instance, the walls may look rather drab at the moment, in which case you might opt for a striped or subtly patterned wallpaper, a special paint technique that introduces texture in the form of broken color, or an embossed wallpaper that can either be painted or be left as it is. Alternatively, you may decide to keep the walls fairly plain but cover them with collections of paintings, plates, or textiles.

The floor is another area that needs careful treatment. Surfaces like ceramic, cork, or slate tiles, wooden floorboards, and parquet or wood-strip flooring all have their own distinctive textures. Here, too, these hard textures are set off perfectly by soft textures such as a few well-placed rugs or mats.

An effective way to break up the floor space is to introduce a few objects with an interesting hard texture, such as wicker baskets, a colonial chair, wooden tables, or small upholstered footstools. Alternatively, if you want a natural, rough-looking floor covering, you might choose coir or rush matting, which has plenty of texture and looks terrific when covered with a few well-placed rugs.

Consider the fabrics you use too. Although these are, by definition, soft-textured there is still a world of difference between various textiles. For instance, heavy fabrics such as velvet and tartan have a dense, matte texture that soaks up the light and provides a rich, luxurious atmosphere. Woven fabrics, such as brocades and jacquards, have a raised surface texture but retain an atmosphere of luxury. More lightweight fabrics, such as cottons and ginghams, have a slight grain which looks good when seen in daylight, while there are some fabrics, such as glazed chintzes and silks, that have a shiny surface texture. You can also choose fabrics with a highly complex texture, such as epinglé and lace.

The character of this rustic farmhouse setting stems from many different textures working together – shiny plates are set against the powdery limewash of rough stone walls, while a woolen throw and a linen pillow are tossed onto a chair.

Looking through into the bedroom, more textures are visible, including old wooden floorboards beneath a wrought iron bed that is decked with cotton bed linen and delicate muslin drapes.

THE INTERPLAY OF PATTERN AND TEXTURE

The photograph below shows the fabrics and wallpapers used for the decoration of the living room which is shown opposite and in the photograph on pages 22–23. Each element in the scheme has a different pattern and texture, but they all coordinate through a similar use of the colors russet and gold.

The patterns are diverse yet designed to work together. The simple, star-shaped woodblock design of the russet wallpaper is contrasted with the large-scale, multicolored traditional floral used for the curtains and large armchair. A smaller-scale floral of a single etched rose scattered on an off-white background covers a smaller chair, pillows, and the decoupage table. The ticking stripe that covers the sofa adds a further pattern and a contemporary twist to the

scheme. Finally, the chenille fabric introduces a depth of color and a woven jacquard pattern.

The fabrics were also chosen for their different textures, and this is what gives the room its elegance – from the linen and cotton weave of the large-scale floral and the rich textures of the jacquard chenille and the pompoms to the finer textures of the herringbone weave ticking stripe, the wallpaper, and the tassels.

When starting to make choices for a decorating scheme, it is useful to gather different swatches and lay them out together, as here. It is the best way to see if all the elements will work together or not. If something clashes, then swap it for a different swatch.

The swatches below were the starting point of the decorating scheme for the living room opposite.

The photograph below shows the decorating scheme for the wooden beachhouse opposite and on pages 82–83. The starting points of this scheme were the pretty floral print called Cornflower Stripe and the existing painted tongue-and-groove walls. The floral design is quite contemporary, combining delicate botanical flowers with a soft chambray blue stripe. The cornflower motif is used for a small-scale, all-over pattern printed on country decorator cotton. These two florals are contrasted with a simple woven gingham, plain white, and chambray blue linen, for a fresh seaside mood.

The textures in this decorating scheme are simpler and more rustic than those used in the elegant faded florals living room. The translucency of the muslin, the simplicity of the wooden walls and gingham, and the natural texture of the linen combine successfully with the chambray blue in this timeless seaside house. The thick cotton throw and heavyweight woven jacquard in cream add depth to the scheme and therefore make it cozier, though in the final scheme these two fabrics were replaced by slipcovers that were made from towels (for summer) or blankets (for winter).

The inspiration for the schemes in both of these rooms was fabric, but there are many other possible starting points for a room scheme, from the character of the house or the function of the room to a favorite piece of furniture or personal collection. Decorating a room with a certain season in mind, as in our winter white dining room on pages 40–41 or our harvest room on pages 64–65, is a particularly good way to choose harmonious schemes in which all the elements work well together. In fact, once you've found your starting point and chosen the decorative theme, you'll probably find that the patterns and textures, as well as the colors, fall into place naturally.

The fabrics below were collected together to decide the decorating scheme for the kitchen in the beach house shown opposite.

CHAPTER TWO

Living Rooms

For many people, the living room is one of the most important rooms in the house. Not only is it a room in which you relax, but it is also the main room in which you entertain, so it has to fulfill two functions.

The amount of available light and the times of day that you use the living room will also influence the way you decorate the room. For example, if you only use the room in the evenings, you might choose decorations and colors that make it especially cozy and welcoming, such as richly textured fabrics like velvets and damasks and shades of brick, russet, and warm golds, as used in the living room on pages 22–23. On the other hand, if you use it during the day you will want to make the most of the available light and choose colors that reflect as much of the daylight as possible – such as creams, pale blues, and yellows or soft greens – as well as light, fresh fabrics like cottons, ginghams, and chintzes.

Even if you have a family room or large kitchen, you will still probably use your living room a great deal, so choose colors, patterns, and textures that are easy to live with. If you are decorating the living room from scratch you can decide what the main focal point will be and plan the rest of your decorations accordingly – a magnificent Oriental carpet, perhaps; a luxurious sofa; a favorite painting or print; an antique textile to hang on a wall; or opulent drapes puddling onto the floor.

However, most people have to accommodate existing pieces of furniture, such as a sofa and armchairs. If you are bored with the upholstery, make slipcovers or liven them up with a collection of plain or patterned throws. If you do not like the shape of a particular

A collection of cranberry and gilded antique glasses on the mantelpiece of our traditional living room (see pages 22–23) adds a rich texture and sparkle, echoing the russet and gold color scheme of the room.

armchair or sofa but find it comfortable, consider re-covering it in a different fabric, which will completely change its character and appearance. For example, for a chair that is too narrow, choose a fabric with a vertical pattern that draws the eye outward or a fabric with a raised texture. Or simply cover the chair with a bulky throw.

Clever choice of pillows also makes a big difference to the existing seating as it provides a way of introducing areas of intense pattern and color. Cut up antique carpets or old kilims that are falling apart and use the areas that are still in good condition to make exotic pillow covers.

(Both also make excellent coverings for foot-stools and ottomans.) Liven up plain pillows with interesting trimmings, such as tassels, braids, contrasting pipings, and beads. Needle-point pillows that you have stitched yourself are a lovely addition to any room, especially the living room, and will give a room a unique character that is entirely your own.

Throughout the room, combining different fabric patterns is the key to a subtle and original decorative scheme. You can mix patterned fabrics with plains, linens with elaborate colorful florals, or bold stripes with textured chenilles for a rich, ecletic look.

DECORATIVE TREATMENTS FOR WALLS

Paint and wallpaper both look good in living rooms. Broken paint treatments, such as rag-rolling and dragging, are especially decorative in rooms that are used during the day because the daylight will accentuate the texture of the walls. However, if you only use the room at night, very subtle paint treatments may not be noticeable in the artificial light, in which case you might prefer a patterned wallpaper. Wallpapers can sometimes make a room look more inviting than painted walls. Stripes, florals, and very subtle, simple patterns all look good in living rooms, or, if you prefer a lavish scheme, you might choose a very decorative paper.

Unpatterned wallpaper is another possibility. Colorwash papers, which have the soft texture of a glazed paint finish, look very smart, particularly when combined with a plain colorwash

border in a contrasting shade. Wallpaper patterned with colorwash stripes is also available. Either of these makes a good background for floral upholstery or curtains.

Embossed paper provides a means of introducing subtle pattern and texture, and because it is painted after hanging, you have an unlimited choice of colors. Embossed paper was originally designed for the lower portion of the wall, but it does not have to be restricted to this area.

Whether you choose paint or paper, the living room is an ideal place to display your favorite paintings, drawings, and photographs. A richly colored wallpaper or paint effect can be a superb background for a group of prints or watercolors in gold frames. Give a collection of disparate paintings a cohesive theme by choosing similar frames and grouping them.

CONCENTRATING ON PATTERN

Use pattern to add atmosphere to your living room, be it a sense of drama and excitement or a feeling of coziness and peace. Although the walls are the largest surfaces in any room, the patterns of the textiles used in the room are just as important. Curtains, upholstery, and carpets are the most crucial, but pillows, throws, lampshades, wall hangings, curtain tiebacks, and valances bring in pattern too.

You may wish to contrast just one very strong design with bold plain fabrics, or you may decide to pile pattern upon pattern. If you do combine patterns, remember that they need to be related in color and feeling. In addition, be aware of any other elements of pattern in the room, such as a beamed ceiling, decorative plasterwork, an elaborate crown molding, an inlaid table, or herringbone-patterned flooring.

CONCENTRATING ON TEXTURE

Whatever the style of your living room, it will only come alive when you introduce plenty of texture. The textiles, floor covering, and wall treatment you choose will all have their own textures but you can introduce further areas of texture in small, subtle ways. If you have a fireplace in the living room, fill the grate with a carefully arranged selection of logs during the times of year that the fire is not lit. In a contemporary room, arrange the logs end-on to make a visually appealing pattern of irregular circles. Baskets of logs also look good, especially if you scatter a few bunches of dried lavender on top – the lavender will release a lovely aroma when put on the fire.

Add texture to walls with the lovely faded colors and intricate stitchwork of antique samplers. Use side tables to display collections of cherished objects, such as antique cups and saucers, family photographs, antique glasses, tiny enamel pillboxes, or beautiful bowls. Large,

shallow brass dishes look wonderful filled with a collection of pine cones of various sizes, particularly if you add a few iridescent marbles that catch the light.

This detail shows the pleasing contrast between the gloss of glazed chintz and the slightly broken texture of apple green colorwash wallpaper.

FADED FLORALS
LIVING ROOM

The rich textures and warm, russet and gold tones of this living room make it instantly welcoming, comfortable, and relaxing. It has the aura of faded elegance that is such an essential part of classic English style – when you look at the photograph you can almost hear the measured ticking of a clock and the crackle of logs burning in the fireplace.

The main patterns in the room are equally classic – the elegant stripes on the sofa and the various florals on the pillows and armchairs. Although the florals are contemporary, they have an antique, slightly faded look that enhances the room's sense of timeless elegance. The wallpaper features a simple, woodblocked pattern of stylized gold stars on a russet background which is subtle enough not to fight with the other patterns in the room yet strong enough to make an impact.

The colors of the scheme were chosen for their warmth and autumnal hues. This is the sort of room that really comes into its own in the winter months, when a log fire is lit and the low afternoon sun filters through the window.

The autumn sunlight sets off the warm tones of russet and gold and the elegant faded floral fabrics in this classic English-style living room.

CONTEMPORARY TWISTS

At first glance the room has a very traditional appearance, but when you examine it more closely you realize that several of the decorating ideas have been given an unexpected, contemporary twist.

For example, a great deal of care has been taken to make the pillows on the sofa and armchairs as interesting as possible – some are trimmed with beads, tassels, or buttons, while a russet pillow in figured chenille fabric, which is a classic choice, has been given a bobble fringe in clashing orange and pink colors.

The decoupage treatment of the table takes conventional decoupage one step further by using cut-outs from one wallpaper pasted onto a background of another wallpaper. The drape tiebacks look perfectly traditional but are made from lengths of chenille twisted around each other and finished with a huge tassel made from

fabric. The mirror frame has been gilded to reveal the rough grain of the underlying wood, which is an interesting twist on most gilded mirror frames, which have an ornate raised pattern. And the herringbone-woven ticking stripe on the sofa is a contemporary complement to the traditional floral linen fabrics.

Other accessories and small items in the room continue the color theme of russet and gold and also the combination of the traditional with the contemporary, while providing lovely textural contrasts. The floral fabric on the Queen Anne chair matches the drapes, while the small armchair is covered in a simple floral print of roses, which also appears as a wallpaper on the decoupage table. The collection of cranberry and gilded antique glasses on the mantelpiece, with its hard, glittering surfaces, contrasts with the soft chenille fabrics used in the room.

COVERED OTTOMAN

The rather grand ottoman shown in the photograph opposite originally had a cracked and worn leather surface and was something of an eyesore. Now, having received a simple overhaul, it can proudly take its place in any living room. The same technique can be used to give a facelift to a footstool.

The cover, in a woven russet-colored jacquard chenille, piped with gold chenille, can easily be removed for cleaning. The chenille makes the ottoman look very traditional, as would a floral

pattern, elegant stripes, or tartan. If you wanted to give it a contemporary feel you could use one fabric for the fitted top portion and a contrasting pattern for the pleated skirt. To accentuate the eastern origins of the pouffe, you could cover it with an Indian print, a rich paisley, or a fabric with a kilim pattern.

Although the trimming used on the cover of this ottoman is piping, you could use cord, braid, tassels, pompoms, braided embroidery floss, ribbons, or rope instead.

YOU WILL NEED

Ottoman

Fabric such as russet-colored woven
jacquard chenille for cover

Contrasting fabric such as gold woven
jacquard chenille for piping

Matching sewing thread

Piping cord

MEASURING

To make the cover, cut a circle the size of the top plus 1in (2.5cm) for a seam allowance and ease.

Cut a strip with a width that is slightly less than half the height of the ottoman, plus 1in (2.5cm) for seam allowances, and a length that is the distance around the middle of the ottoman plus 2½in (6.5cm) for seam allowances and ease.

Cut a second strip with a width slightly more than half the height of the ottoman plus ½in (1.25cm) for a seam allowance and 1¼in (3cm) for a hem, and a length that is just under twice the length of the other strip.

Cut enough bias binding (see page 44, step 6) to go around the ottoman twice plus 5in (13cm) for seam allowances and ease.

1 Taking ½in (1.25cm) seams, join the ends of both strips to form two rings. The smaller one should fit comfortably around the ottoman.

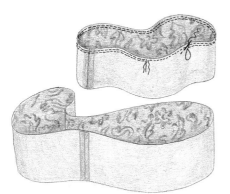

2 Cover the piping cord with the bias binding (see page 44, step 7). With the zipper foot on the machine, and with raw edges even, stitch the piping around the right side of the circle, along a seamline ½in (1.25cm) from the edge, clipping into the seam allowance on the curves. Also stitch piping around the lower edge of the smaller ring. Trim both seams.

3 Still with the zipper foot on the machine, and with right sides together, join the smaller ring to the circle, taking a ½in (1.25cm) seam. Trim the seam and clip the curves.

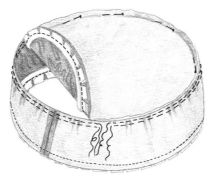

4 Make small inverted box pleats around the top edge of the larger ring, adjusting the spacing between them until it fits the lower edge of the smaller ring. Baste the pleats in place. With the zipper foot on the machine and with right sides together, join the larger ring to the smaller ring around these edges, taking a ½in (1.25cm) seam. Check for fit, and turn up ¼in (6mm) and then 1in (2.5cm) on the lower edge. Press and stitch. Turn right side out.

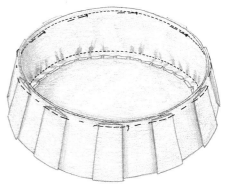

PAINTED PLANTER

The extremely smart planter on the chest of drawers in the photograph shown here is the ideal container for a pot-et-fleur arrangement (growing plants with cut flowers). Its rich gold and deep red paint echoes the main color scheme of the room and, looking at it, you would never imagine that it was originally a tin bath found in a junk shop.

Although it is waterproof, filling the planter with potting compost and plants is not advisable because there will not be any drainage holes for the water. A much better option is to arrange a collection of potted plants (which you have already watered well and allowed to drain) in the planter so that some of the leaves spill over the sides, then add a few jars of fresh flowers if you wish. The sides of the planter will hide the pots from view and you can replace the fresh flowers whenever they start to fade.

1 First remove any rust and dirt, then apply a metal primer. Allow to dry.

2 Mix up the deep red shade using crimson and burnt sienna acrylics to tint the white latex. Dilute it with a little water and polyvinyl acetate. Apply three coats, adding a little ultramarine to the paint for the second and third coats, and allowing it to dry after each coat.

3 Finally, apply a gold paint around the rim and base and on the handles. (To help you paint the stripe around the base, you can stick low-tack masking tape around the top edge of the stripe first, peeling it off very carefully after painting, to prevent it from pulling off the deep red paint.) Varnish.

YOU WILL NEED

OLD GALVANIZED TIN CONTAINER

METAL PRIMER

ACRYLIC PAINTS IN CRIMSON, BURNT SIENNA, AND ULTRAMARINE

LATEX PAINT IN WHITE

POLYVINYL ACETATE SIZING

WATER-BASED PAINT IN PALE GOLD

SATIN FINISH ACRYLIC VARNISH

DECOUPAGE TABLE

YOU WILL NEED

POLYVINYL ACETATE SIZING
STRIPED, FLORAL, AND STARRY WALLPAPERS
(OR PATTERNS OF YOUR OWN CHOICE)
WALLPAPER PASTE
ACRYLIC OR POLYURETHANE VARNISH,
TINTED WITH RAW UMBER ACRYLIC PAINT

Decoupage, which uses images cut from pieces of paper, has long been a classic way to decorate pieces of furniture and smaller items such as mats and trays. The aim is to make it appear that the cut-outs have been painted on, and the many layers of varnish that are traditionally applied on top help foster this impression.

Most decoupage consists of cut-outs pasted onto a painted surface, sometimes singly or in small groups and sometimes in a complicated

collage. For this table, however, a very different approach was used, in which cut-out images were pasted onto a background of wallpaper. The wood is allowed to show all around the edge of each surface, framing the paper. The two patterns – the stripes and the flowers – are the wallpaper versions of the fabrics used on the sofa and one of the armchairs respectively.

Using wallpaper for decoupage like this is an excellent way to disguise a table that is less than perfect in its natural state. Panels of the striped wallpaper have been pasted onto the wood of the tabletop with small cut-out sprigs of roses and leaves glued over it. Narrow strips of a different-colored version of the starry wallpaper that covers the walls of the living room have been pasted down the center of each table leg.

You could easily adapt this idea for a smaller or larger table, a tray, a chest of drawers, a wooden trunk, a large box, a filing cabinet, a cupboard door, or a mirror frame.

1 Rub down the table with medium sandpaper, then apply sizing (diluted with two parts water to one part polyvinyl acetate) to improve adhesion of the paper. Allow to dry.

2 Plan the design before beginning to cut or paste, then cut out the paper. Use a ruler and carpenter's square to insure the lines are straight and the corners square, and either a mat knife

and cutting mat or a pair of sharp, pointed scissors to help you cut the paper accurately.

3 Apply wallpaper paste to the pieces for the bottom layer, making sure it goes right to the edges. Position carefully, using a cloth or sponge to smooth the pieces from the center outward so that no air bubbles are trapped. Remove any excess paste.

4 Allow to dry, then paste the flowers and leaves over the tabletop in the same way.

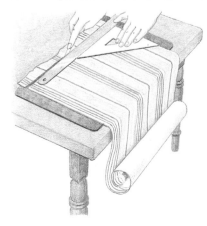

5 For an attractively aged look, tint the varnish with raw umber acrylic paint. Apply several thin coats of varnish, allowing it to dry between coats. If desired, continue applying coats of varnish, rubbing down lightly with fine steel wool after every two coats.

DECORATED PILLOWS

There are many different pillow treatments in this living room, from the simple to the more elaborate. In the photograph of the room on pages 22–23, the matching pillows in the armchairs flanking the fireplace are made from the ticking stripe herringbone-weave fabric used for the sofa. The front of each cover is made by cutting four identically patterned right-angled triangles and sewing them together into a square so that the stripes form a border pattern. A tassel is sewn on at the point where the right angles meet in the middle. On page 24, a woven chenille pillow has been trimmed with exotic colored pompoms around the edges.

In the photograph above, a gold chenille pillow has been decorated with tortoiseshell beads sewn on in clusters to look like flowers. Single ceramic beads have also been sewn onto the cushion at random.

In the same photograph, the elegant pillow with a scalloped front opening is fastened with what look like two large strawberries. In fact, they are two large, fabric buttons that have been embroidered with tiny cross stitches and edged with small metallic beads. The four corners of the pillow are trimmed with lavish gold silk tassels. Step-by-step directions for making this pillow follow.

YOU WILL NEED

FABRIC FOR COVER SUCH AS A FLORAL LINEN

LINING FABRIC FOR COVER (OPTIONAL – SEE STEP 3)

CONTRASTING FABRIC FOR BUTTONS

MATCHING SEWING THREAD

FUSIBLE INTERFACING

LARGE COVERED BUTTON KITS

EMBROIDERY FLOSS

BEADS

TASSELS OR SILK THREAD

PILLOW FORM

1 First make the beaded buttons. Cut a fabric circle for each button, then embroider some tiny cross stitches on the right side of the fabric circle using embroidery floss. Cover the button with the embroidered fabric, following the manufacturer's directions. Finally, sew beads all around the edge of the covered button.

2 Next make your scallop template. Cut a piece of paper the same width as the pillow form. Use a compass to draw circles all the same size along the edge of the paper corresponding to the cushion width. Position the outer edges of the circles so they just touch the edges of the paper, and space the circles about 1¼in (3cm) apart. Decide how shallow you'd like them to be, and draw a line to indicate where they will end. Cut out the template.

3 Now cut out your fabric pieces for the pillow cover. For the back, cut a square 1in (2.5cm) larger each way than your pillow form. For the front, cut a rectangle to the width of the square and to a depth of half this measurement plus 1¼in (3cm). Cut another rectangle to the width of the square and to a depth of half this measurement plus the depth of the template plus ½in (1.25cm). Cut a third rectangle to the same dimensions as the second, either from the same fabric or from a lining fabric. On the small rectangle, turn under ¼in (6mm) along one long edge and stitch.

4 Place the template along one long edge of a large rectangle, on the wrong side, so that the edges are ½in (1.25cm) from the fabric edges. Draw around the template, extending the horizontal line on each side as shown. Place the two large rectangles with right sides together. Pin and baste around the scallops but not the gaps between them.

5 Cut a 1in (2.5cm) strip of the main fabric on the straight grain. After stitching, it will be cut into segments, one for each button loop, the length of which will depend on the size of your buttons. When shaped into a loop it should just fit over a button, with a ½in (1.25cm) seam allowance at each end. Fold the long raw edges in almost to the center, then fold in half lengthwise. Press and stitch along one long edge. Cut into segments.

6 Form each segment into a loop and insert it into one of the gaps between scallops, with the loop flat and the raw ends projecting ½in (1.25cm) beyond the marked stitching line. Baste firmly in place, then check that the button will fit through the loop.

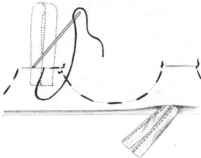

7 Stitch along the marked line, pivoting at the corners and catching the loops in the seam. Trim the seam and clip into the seam allowances on the curves and at the corners. Remove the basting. Turn right side out and press. Top-stitch along the scalloped edge.

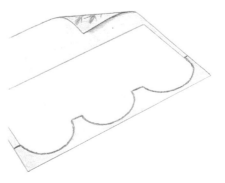

8 Lay the fabric square face up on a flat surface. Place the scalloped piece face down on top of it, with the three raw edges even. Place the other rectangle on top of that, also face down, with the long raw edge along the remaining raw edge of the back.

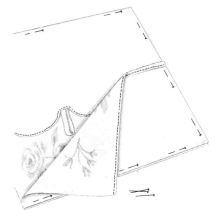

The finished edges of the two rectangles will overlap in the center.

9 Stitch around all four edges of the square. Trim the seam and trim off the corners. Turn right side out and press. Sew the beaded buttons onto the underneath front piece, beneath the corresponding loops.

10 Sew on tassels at the corners. If you wish to make your own, wind thread or yarn around two pieces of cardboard until it is the desired thickness of the tassel. Tie at the top with another piece of yarn. Insert the scissors blade between the pieces of cardboard and cut the yarn at the bottom. Slide the cardboard out. Wrap the lengths of yarn over the knot and arrange so it is covered. Using another length of thread, bind about a fifth of the way down. Thread the end through a needle and take it through the tassel and out the center of the top, then use it to sew the tassels onto the cushion cover at each corner.

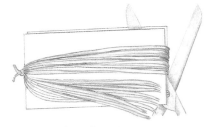

11 Insert the pillow form through the opening, and button to close.

DRAPERY TIEBACKS

Drapes can be made to look more elegant with tiebacks. Using tiebacks also increases the amount of light that enters the room and accents the colors, patterns, and textures of the drapes themselves.

You can choose from many different types of tiebacks, including hooked metal arms; stiffened fabric tiebacks decorated with a variety of trimmings such as self-piping, cord, fringes, pompoms, or bows; thick cords trimmed with tassels; or jute, braid, chain, or even beads.

Fabric tiebacks can be made from the same fabric as the curtains or drapes, or from a contrasting fabric – perhaps a checked tieback for a striped drapery, or a gingham one if a cheerful floral print has been used for the curtains.

If the fabric for the valance is different from that used for the drapes, you could use the valance fabric for the tiebacks.

The tieback shown opposite is made from two padded tubes of woven jacquard chenille in russet and old gold twisted together to form a soft rope. It is trimmed with a huge tassel made from russet chenille and a lighter-weight fabric in the gold shade. The two fabrics are cut into six-pointed stars, stitched together, and then wrapped over padding and fastened with a band of gold chenille.

A variation of this idea would be to braid three colors together, either trimming them with a store-bought tassel in one of the colors or leaving the tieback unadorned.

YOU WILL NEED

FOR THE FABRIC TASSELS
FABRIC IN TWO COLORS, SUCH AS WOVEN
JACQUARD CHENILLE IN RUSSET AND
OLD GOLD
LIGHTWEIGHT FABRIC IN GOLD
MATCHING SEWING THREAD
POLYESTER FIBERFILL (LOOSE OR BATTING)
1 CURTAIN RING FOR EACH TASSEL

FOR THE TWISTED CHENILLE TIEBACKS
FABRIC IN TWO COLORS, SUCH AS WOVEN
JACQUARD CHENILLE IN RUSSET AND
OLD GOLD
MATCHING SEWING THREAD
LIGHTWEIGHT BATTING
(OPTIONAL – SEE STEP 1)
2 CURTAIN RINGS FOR EACH TIEBACK
1 HOOK FOR EACH TIEBACK

Fabric tassels

1 To make one fabric tassel, cut out a six-pointed star about 15–18in (38–45cm) deep from the russet chenille and another from the lighter-weight fabric. Stitch them with right sides together around the edges, taking a ¼in (6mm) seam and leaving an opening in one edge. Clip the corners, trim off the

points, turn right side out, and press. Slipstitch the opening.

2 Cut a 1¾in (4.5cm) wide band of gold chenille long enough to wrap around the tassels. Turn under ¼in (6mm) along all the raw edges. Fold it in half lengthwise, and stitch across the ends and down the side.

3 Make a ball of stuffing or batting and place the fabric star over it, chenille side up. Wrap the fabric around it and bind tightly under the stuffing with the narrow band. Hand sew the ends of the band together. Sew a ring to the center of the tassel top.

Twisted chenille tiebacks

1 For each tieback, cut a 3in (7.5cm) wide strip of each fabric. Decide the length by holding a tape measure loosely around the drapery, then adding 1in (2.5cm). If you are using a thin fabric or if you want the tiebacks to be quite fat, also cut one 1in (2.5cm) wide strip of batting for each tieback, to provide padding.

2 If you are not padding the tiebacks, fold the strips in half lengthwise, with right sides together, and stitch a ½in (1.25cm) seam along the long edge and across one end. Trim the seam, turn right side out, and press. Turn in the raw edges at the other end and slip-stitch neatly in place.

3 If you *are* padding them, turn under ½in (1.25cm) on one long and two short edges; lay the batting on the wrong side of the fabric strip, and roll the fabric around it, starting with the raw edge. Slipstitch along the folded edge.

4 Hand sew the end of one tube on top of the other, sewing a curtain ring between them so that it projects

beyond the end. Twist the tubes around each other and hand sew the other two ends together, with another curtain ring between them.

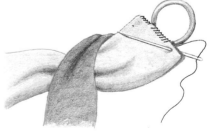

5 Screw a hook into the wall behind the drapery. Wrap the tieback around the drapery and slip the rings over the hook on the wall.

GILDED FRAME

For a change from the traditional molded look of most gilded objects, this idea is an excellent one to copy. Use it either for a mirror frame, as shown here, or for a picture frame. If you cannot find a suitable frame with a rough wooden surface, you could commission a picture framer to make one especially for you. In that case, emphasize that you want the frame to be made from a rough-grained, open-textured wood, and that you do not want it to be sanded down. This frame is made from 4 x 1in (10 x 2.5cm) sawn boards.

If you are decorating a picture frame you will obviously need to remove the picture. If you will be gilding a mirror frame, cut a piece of cardboard to fit the mirror's surface exactly.

Traditional gilding involves applying transfer metal leaf or metallic powder to an oil-based varnish known as goldsize. A much easier method, however, is simply to brush on a gold paint or gold cream. The paint and the wood enhance each other because the rough texture of the wood softens the gilt while the sheen of the gilt emphasizes the texture.

Before you start, treat any knots to prevent the resin from eventually discoloring the finish. Follow this with an acrylic primer. When it is dry, very lightly rub down the surface to provide a key. (Don't overdo it or you'll lose the rough texture.) Now apply two coats of gold paint, allowing them to dry between coats, and then rub with a wax polish.

CHAPTER THREE

Dining Rooms

One of the great pleasures when decorating a dining room is the knowledge that it is used for a specific purpose. This means that you can concentrate on the room's single function rather than having to take into account a number of often conflicting considerations.

The dining table is likely to be the largest piece of furniture, and therefore the focal point of the room, so you may wish to plan the rest of your design around it. If the table is made of wood, the patina, finish, and grain will create instant pattern, texture, and a sense of warmth, which you can emphasize in the way you decorate the rest of the dining room.

A metal or glass-topped table, on the other hand, will have a completely different character and will have to be treated accordingly. Warmth and coziness can be introduced with softening elements such as upholstered dining chairs with rounded tops, a tapestry or quilt on the walls, or kilims and rugs in wonderfully faded colors on the floor.

It is very important for the atmosphere in a dining room to be relaxing and convivial. Color plays a vital role in creating a suitable atmosphere. Reds and oranges will provide a rich, glowing ambience, while neutral shades, warm blues, and pale greens will create a more calming and peaceful atmosphere.

Antique creamware on an oak hutch continues the theme of white on white texture and pattern in our rustic dining room (see page 41). The characteristic openwork piercing of the plate rims, the twisted handles, and the intricate relief decoration of the creamware are set off beautifully by the dark wood, making the addition of any other color completely unnecessary.

CHOOSING PATTERNS

Pattern is an important consideration here. Stripes are a classic choice for dining rooms, especially if they are narrow, because they are elegant and they introduce pattern without being obtrusive. If you prefer, use a textured wallpaper up to chair rail height with plain walls above. You can also use a number of different paint techniques on the walls to create broken color – glazing, dragging, sponging, and rag-rolling will all diffuse the color of the paint and create interesting textures. If you want a beautiful, ornate

wallpaper, balance it with plain or striped curtains. Because a dining room is not a place where one spends a lot of time, it can be more elaborate or dramatic than the living room.

You can be much more flexible when choosing the fabric for the drapes and for any seat covers. If you have opted for a fairly plain treatment for the walls, you can introduce plenty of pattern and texture with the drapes. Florals, stripes, and checks all work well in dining rooms, or you could swath the windows in lengths of muslin.

For a stylish look, choose one fabric for the valance and a completely different one for the draperies themselves. This treatment is most successful when each fabric contains the same or very similar colors, otherwise it can look rather haphazard.

If your dining chairs have wooden seats, fitting padded covers or knife-edge cushions held in place with ties will add comfort and introduce further color and pattern. Choose one fabric for all the seat covers or use a selection of fabrics linked by either color or pattern. If you have an antique dining table, an alternative to expensive antique chairs is a set of cheap kitchen or garden chairs with fabric slipcovers (see pages 132–133).

In our dining room (page 41) the chandelier with its green and red glass ornaments brings a jewel-like quality and elegance to what is essentially a simple decorating scheme.

DRESSING THE TABLE

Your dining table may look marvelous just as it is, but if you prefer to cover it with a tablecloth, your choice will be dictated by the colors and patterns of the rest of the room. A large damask tablecloth, a ready-made plain or patterned tablecloth, or one you have made yourself from a length of sheeting are all possibilities. Alternatively, add texture and an element of surprise to the room by covering the table with an antique chenille cloth, an old bedspread, or even an antique rug, any of which can be removed at mealtimes.

If the surface of the table is in poor condition, a coat of paint can transform it. Painted geometric patterns or a stenciled or stamped border around the edge of the tabletop or around the sides can make an inexpensive table a beautiful focal point of the room.

FURNITURE AND FLOOR COVERINGS

If there is enough room, a couple of armchairs or even a sofa will help to create a relaxed atmosphere. Upholster them in a fabric that complements the drapes, or cover them with throws or antique patchwork quilts for a more informal look. You might want to add a different piece of furniture instead, such as a bookcase, a sideboard, or a desk. To liven up a display cabinet, you could line the back with wallpaper or an attractive marbled paper.

Coir or sisal matting or wall-to-wall carpets are practical choices for dining rooms. If you like the effect of polished wooden floorboards and a few rugs, avoid placing any rugs with curling edges between the doorway and the table to prevent you from catching your feet on them.

LIGHTING

The dining table must be carefully lit with an appropriate fixture. Over the table, you could have a pendant fixture, a sparkling chandelier, or recessed down-lights. Install a dimmer switch so you can vary the light from bright and functional to soft and intimate.

To prevent shadowy corners, provide soft background light with small, unobtrusive up-lights, wall lights, or table lamps.

Candlelight, though not very practical for everyday use, is the most relaxing and intimate choice of all but is best reserved for special occasions. For a romantic look there's no reason why you can't light the whole room with candlelight, using candles in candelabras and wall sconces (or even the floorstanding holders for large candles) as well as candlesticks. Do not leave them unattended when lit, however.

WINTER WHITE DINING ROOM

Texture plays a vital role in the design of this colonial-style dining room, from the white jacquard seat covers to the mirror frame adorned with pine cones, nuts, and seeds. The shades of white with accents of dark green in the room were inspired by the colors and textures of winter – snowflakes, bare trees, ivy, and other evergreens.

The play of light and shade on the textured objects in this room is what makes them look so interesting. Overlaying a neutral color with more of the same is a classic way to introduce layers of texture without making a room look busy or overpowering.

The basic elements of the room have deliberately been kept simple – a flooring of coir matting, a plain embossed wallpaper below the chair rail with painted walls above, and nineteenth-century Windsor chairs whose curved backs form their own patterns, especially when seen against their white seat covers.

All the fabrics are cottons – the curtains are made from a white, roughly woven Indian cotton trimmed with a double row of bottle-green tape, while the seat covers are made from an antique jacquard bedspread in a pattern of white-on-white.

The color has been kept very simple in this room to allow the variety and layers of different textures, inspired by cold, crisp winters in the countryside, to feature more strongly. It creates a superb setting for Christmas entertaining but is not so overtly festive as to make it unsuitable for entertaining all through the winter.

The wooden fireplace has been given a rough coat of white paint over a dark grey undercoat, while the brush strokes have deliberately been kept patchy to enhance the overall texture.

With the exception of the metal chandelier decorated with green and red glass ornaments, most of the other decorative objects in the room are made from wood and feature a selection of white motifs reminiscent of snowflakes. A small wooden wall cupboard has been stamped with a white pattern. A long wooden trough filled with plants has been placed beneath the main window and has also been decorated with white stamping; and three antique lace mats, their shapes also resembling snowflakes, have been given rustic wooden frames and hung side by side on the wall (see page 46).

Continuing the white-on-white textural theme, the hutch is adorned with a beautiful collection of antique creamware (see pages 36–37). Further texture is introduced through the mirror frame with its decoration of nuts, leaves, and cinnamon sticks, and the rustic candlesticks made from wooden branches.

WHITE JACQUARD SEAT COVERS

Seat covers can be made from all kinds of fabric, from heavy velvets to pretty chintz or elegant stripes. These six covers are made from two antique bedspreads in heavy cotton. They were chosen for their jacquard patterns, which, despite being white-on-white, provide a lovely, subtle texture. The edges of the bedspreads, which featured a different pattern, have been used for the ties and the skirts of the seat covers. Not only does this do away with the need to make hems, but it also looks much neater and more delicate. The seam joining the cover to the skirt is emphasized with self-piping.

The seat covers on pages 72–73 were made in the same way as the ones shown here but have a very different appearance. A comparison of the two illustrates how patterns and colors seem to change the shape of an object.

Once you have started cutting up old, damaged bedspreads to make chair covers, you will probably not want to stop there. Old tablecloths, curtains whose edges have faded in the sun, tea towels, tray cloths, and even sheets bearing patterns that adapt easily to the dining room make attractive cushions and seat covers. You can also plunder pieces of clothing, such as old shawls, scarves, shirts, and skirts. A set of seat covers with different patterns on each, but featuring the same colors to give them a cohesive look, is charming.

The beauty of this idea is that you give new life to a piece that could otherwise no longer be used. Sometimes you will have to cut away quite large areas that have been damaged by moths, exposure to sunlight, or general wear-and-tear. That need not matter, however, because you can stitch the remaining pieces into a patchwork, perhaps combining one fabric with another – strips of a delicate damask tablecloth could be teamed with a soft, faded floral print, or a

FABRIC OR CENTER OF OLD COTTON
BEDSPREAD, FOR TOP
FABRIC OR EDGE OF THE SAME OLD COTTON
BEDSPREAD, FOR SKIRT
MATCHING SEWING THREAD
PIPING CORD
HEAVYWEIGHT BATTING

1 First make the pattern for the top of the cover. Lay a piece of paper on the chair. Fold it over the edges of the seat onto the back. Draw around the seat using these creases as guide lines. So that the pattern will be symmetrical, fold the paper in half from front to back and cut out the shape as near as possible to the pencil lines on both halves. Put it back on the seat to check the fit, and adjust if necessary. Mark the positions of the two outer struts.

2 Use the pattern to cut two pieces of fabric, adding a ½in (1.25cm) seam allowance all around. Cut a piece of batting to the same size as the fabric.

3 For the skirt, measure from one outer strut around the seat to the other outer strut. Cut a strip of fabric as long as this measurement plus 13in (32.5cm), and about 6½in (16.5cm) wide. Cut this strip from the edge of the bedspread (if using).

4 Hem the ends of the strip. If it comes from the edge of a bedspread and has an inconspicuous selvage, there is no need to hem the lower edge. Otherwise, turn up a double ¼in (6mm) hem, press, and stitch.

sprigged pattern with stripes. All sorts of patterns can be put together, although they will look best if they are coordinated in some way – be it color or scale of print. Small lengths of fabric can be used to make skirts for seat covers or flanges for cushions. See page 49 for another way of using old textiles.

If you use washable batting, the covers will be washable. The instructions are for making one seat cover.

5 Form a 3in (7.5cm) inverted pleat at each front corner – in other words, two 1½in (4cm) knife pleats facing each other. Baste across the top of each of the pleats.

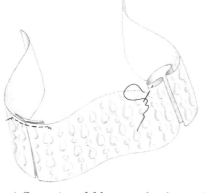

6 Cut strips of fabric on the diagonal for bias binding. The strips should be wide enough to fit around the piping cord with a ½in (1.25cm) seam allowance on each edge.

7 Join the ends of the binding on the straight grain as shown, making a

strip long enough to pipe all around the seat cover.

8 Wrap the binding around the piping and stitch close to the cord. With the zipper foot on the machine and raw edges even, stitch the piping around the edge of one seat piece on the right side, clipping into the piping seam allowance at the corners.

9 With right sides together and raw edges even, baste the top edge of the skirt around the cover, starting and stopping at the outer struts.

10 Cut four 3 x 8½in (7.5 x 21.5cm) strips of fabric. On each, turn under

¼in (6mm) on both long sides and one end, and press. Fold in half lengthwise, wrong sides together, and stitch across the turned-under end and down the side of the folded strip.

11 Place two strips on top of the skirt, on either side of one outer strut, with raw edges even. Baste in place. Repeat for the other two strips and the other outer strut.

12 Place the other cover piece on top, with right sides together. Lay the batting over the top of that. With the

zipper foot on the machine, stitch through all the layers, taking a ½in (1.25cm) seam and leaving an opening at the back for turning. Trim the seam, cut away the batting within the seam allowance, and clip into the seam allowance on the curves.

13 Turn the cover right side out. Slip-stitch the opening. Remove any visible basting, and press.

TEXTURED MIRROR FRAME

Decorating a plain wooden mirror frame with nuts, pine cones, and leaves is a very easy way to introduce texture and pattern into a room. This mirror frame has been covered with cinnamon sticks, pine cones, bark, twigs, short sprigs of pine needles, bay leaves (chosen because they keep their color and shape as they dry out), walnuts and brazil nuts, all of which were stuck in place with a hot-glue gun. You could use other natural materials for a similar effect, such as shells, driftwood, stones and pebbles, moss, and dried seedheads.

It is important to select items that will not rot or wither. Horse chestnuts, for example, look beautiful when they first fall from the trees but they will wither very quickly.

A hot-glue gun dramatically speeds up the job of gluing on so many pieces. It works particularly well for chunky items like nuts and pine cones. Be careful not to get any hot glue on your fingers, and never leave the glue gun unattended when it is plugged in.

DECORATIVE CHRISTMAS BRANCHES

This simple but striking decoration is a fun idea for a Christmas dining room. Anchor a few interestingly shaped branches in a terra-cotta flowerpot filled with earth or small stones, and cover it with bun moss. Now hang buttons and beads or other small decorations on the branches, as shown here. Use a fine thread so that it will not be noticeable.

FRAMED ANTIQUE PLACE MATS

The rustic wooden frames and textured brown paper on which the collection of antique lace mats shown opposite is mounted accentuate their snowflake-like patterns and textures beautifully. They also emphasize the rusticity of the room. These frames can easily be made by any picture framer. You can look out for old, distressed pieces of wood such as fence posts or driftwood – or distress the frame yourself (see page 118 for the technique).

BRANCH CANDLESTICKS

Candlelight gives a marvelous atmosphere to any room and is particularly useful in dining rooms, where its gentle glow helps guests relax. Even when candles are unlit, they can be an attractive decoration in a room.

The perfect choice for this dining room in which texture is paramount, the candlesticks shown opposite and in the photograph on pages 40–41 are made from branches of birch trees. This gives them a wonderfully rustic quality and an extreme simplicity in which the natural beauty of the wood shines through. They are easy to make from short lengths of branches. Use thick prunings from fruit trees to make very short candlesticks, or buy lengths of unpeeled wood (sold for fencing) to make thicker, taller candlesticks.

The most important point to remember is that the candlesticks must be sturdy enough to bear the weight of a candle without toppling over, otherwise they could be a fire hazard. If in doubt, do not light them – they will still look good. The narrow candlesticks have been given firm bases made from circular slices of a branch but the wider ones are heavy enough to stand by themselves. Insure that the base of the candlestick is completely flat because any bumps or knots in the wood will make it unstable.

Tying a group of candlesticks together with a length of rope or twine, as has been done in this room, not only improves their balance, but also looks dramatic, particularly when each candlestick is a different height and made from a different type of wood. Rope has also been bound around some of the individual candlesticks in order to introduce another natural texture.

Choose branches with interesting bark formations if possible. Silver birch, western larch, firs, and maple are all good choices. Snip off side branches and twigs at the base of the branch; the bumps that are left add visual appeal and maintain its natural, woodsy quality.

To secure the candle to the branch, hammer a headless nail into the top, leaving part of it projecting from the branch. Heat it with a match before spearing a candle onto it. Alternatively, make a holder for the candle from a small cookie cutter that is the same diameter as the candle, gluing it to the top of the branch.

TRIMMED CURTAINS

Ready-made fabric is not the only source of pattern in textiles – you can also create your own patterns by mixing strips of different fabrics or adding special trimmings that complement the main colors or textures in your room. Or use trimmings to outline simple, neutral-colored curtains, as in this dining room where the white curtains might otherwise have disappeared into the off-white walls, especially when viewed from a distance.

The trimmings on these curtains have deliberately been kept plain to match the rest of the room, but if you were decorating a more elaborate room you could use silky piping cord, perhaps stitching it into loops at the corners. This would look particularly attractive on heavy velvet or slubbed silk curtains. The edges of floral curtains could be bound with wide or narrow strips of a fabric that picks out the main color of the pattern.

Another way of introducing extra pattern to curtains is to line them in a complementary or contrasting fabric and then loop them back in such a way that the lining is clearly visible.

YOU WILL NEED

FABRIC

LINING FABRIC

1IN (2.5CM) WIDE TRIM

MATCHING SEWING THREAD

PENCIL PLEAT SELF-STYLING CURTAIN TAPE

1 Cut out a pair of lined curtains in the usual way (see pages 68-69 for the sewn-in lining method), omitting the integral valance and adding 1½in (4cm) to the length for a heading.

2 Starting at the top of the curtain, on the right side of the fabric, pin the trim near the hemline of one side edge. Baste and then stitch along the inner edge of the trim.

3 When you are ready to turn the corner, miter the corner by folding the trim back on itself then folding it down diagonally. Crease along this line with your fingers. Lift up the top layer of the trim and stitch across the crease as shown. Cut away the trim beneath the stitching line. Place the trim near the hemline of the next edge and continue pinning and stitching.

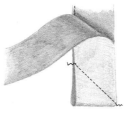

4 Attach the trim along each edge in the same way, until you reach the top on the other side edge. Now stitch the outer edge of the trim. Attach the other border in the same way.

5 Trim 1½in (4cm) off the top edge of the lining. Complete the curtains (see page 69, steps 2, 3, 6, 7, 8, 9), folding the fabric over the lining before covering the raw edge with the tape in step 7. Avoid creating too many pleats on the portion of the heading where the tape is. Keeping it flat will allow the trim to show to full advantage.

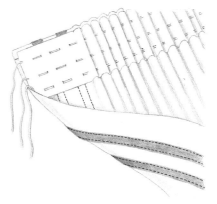

ANTIQUE-TEXTILE PILLOWS

Once upon a time, the best-dressed trays were always adorned with dazzlingly white, starched tray cloths decorated with lace panels, cutwork, or embroidery. However, the days of such elegance and luxury are long gone for most people, who have neither the time nor the patience to keep their table linen in this immaculate condition. As a result, tray cloths, small tablecloths, and once-crisp damask napkins can be found lurking sadly at the back of many a chest of drawers or sideboard. They do not have to stay there, however. Instead, they can be brought out, washed, and converted into a variety of pillows.

Of the two pillows shown on the previous page, the buttoned pillow sham was made from two corners of one of the old jacquard bedspreads used for the seat covers on pages 42–45, so a hem was not necessary. The paneled pillow sham was made from two old tray cloths, which had selvages all around so that here too the edge could be made part of the design, resembling piping. Ordinary fabric can be used too, by modifying the technique.

YOU WILL NEED

FOR BUTTONED PILLOW
FABRIC OR 2 CORNERS OF OLD COTTON JACQUARD BEDSPREAD
MATCHING SEWING THREAD
BUTTONS
CUSHION FORM

FOR PANELED PILLOW
2 TRAY CLOTHS OF THE SAME SIZE
MATCHING SEWING THREAD
ZIPPER
CUSHION FORM

Buttoned pillow

1 Try to adapt the shape of the pillow sham to the textile you are using, utilizing a border or selvage edges if possible. Cut out two fabric pieces, one for the front and one for the back, adding seam/hem allowances all around (see steps 2 and 3).

2 On the opening edge of each piece if there is no selvage, turn under ¼in (6mm) and then 1in (2.5cm). If there is a selvage, there is no need to hem the edge. Make buttonholes in the front piece near the edge.

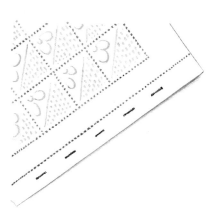

3 If you can't utilize selvages, stitch reversed French seams; first stitch the two pieces with right sides together, taking a ⅛in (3mm) seam, around the three remaining edges; then turn right side out, press the seams, and stitch again ³⁄₁₆in (4–5mm) from the previous seamline, completely enclosing the raw edges. If there is an inconspicuous selvage on one or more edges, sew only the second stage of the French seam along that edge.

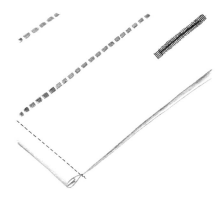

4 Sew buttons to the inside of the remaining edge of the back in line with the buttonholes.

Paneled pillow

1 Fold both tray cloths at each short end as shown, adjusting the folds to suit the design of the border on the tray cloth. Stitch along the fold.

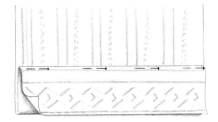

2 Place the cloths with right sides together, and stitch a ½in (1.25cm) seam along the bottom edge. Insert a zipper in this seam, then open it.

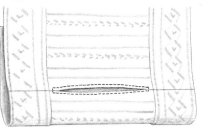

3 Stitch the remaining edges of the two tray cloths as for the buttoned pillow, step 3.

STAMPED CUPBOARD

A good way to brighten up a piece of furniture or apply a simple painted motif to a wall or door is to decorate the surface with hand-blocking. Also known as stamping, this technique gives a charmingly irregular but attractive finish, and it is extremely quick and easy to do. We have used a simple white design for this wooden cupboard and also for the lovely wooden planter by the window on page 43. Choose from the wide selection of rubber and wooden stamps now available, encompassing everything from botanical motifs to geometric patterns. Or make your own stamps, either from a linoleum block or from vegetables such as potatoes, into which you carve your design. (Vegetable stamps can sometimes give a patchy effect, however, because it is difficult for the paint to adhere to the surface, so you may prefer to use one of the other types of stamps.)

Keep the design simple. Not only does this suit the slightly irregular finish that stamps give but it also helps to prevent the paint or printing ink from forming into blobs or filling in the cut-out lines of the design. If you want to create very ornate patterns, use a stencil instead (see page 115). Either printer's ink or paint can be used in the printing; artist's acrylic paint is one of the most effective printing mediums because it dries very fast and has a good color.

When cutting out your own stamps, it is important to use a sharp X-acto knife so you get clean lines. This will also reduce the risk of the blade slipping and cutting your fingers.

YOU WILL NEED

DARK WOOD CUPBOARD
FLAT LATEX GLAZE (OPTIONAL – SEE STEP 1)
WHITE BLOCK-PRINTING COLOR OR ACRYLIC PAINT
ACRYLIC MEDIUM (IF USING ACRYLIC PAINT)
SMALL ROLLER
RUBBER-AND-WOOD, LINOLEUM, OR VEGETABLE STAMP
FLAT ACRYLIC VARNISH (OPTIONAL)

1 Remove any wax or oil-based varnish from the wood, and sand lightly. If the wood is very porous, seal it with flat latex glaze.

2 Pour the white ink or paint into a small, shallow dish. If you are using paint, apply a drop or two of acrylic medium in order to make the paint a more workable consistency.

3 Roll the roller through the ink or paint until it is well absorbed then move the roller over the stamp.

4 Practice first on dark paper to make sure you are using the correct amount and consistency of ink or paint and the right degree of pressure. When you are satisfied, apply the stamp to the cupboard or planter. Allow to dry.

5 If desired, varnish to make the surface waterproof. This is advisable for the planter because of the proximity of wet leaves.

CHAPTER FOUR

Family Rooms

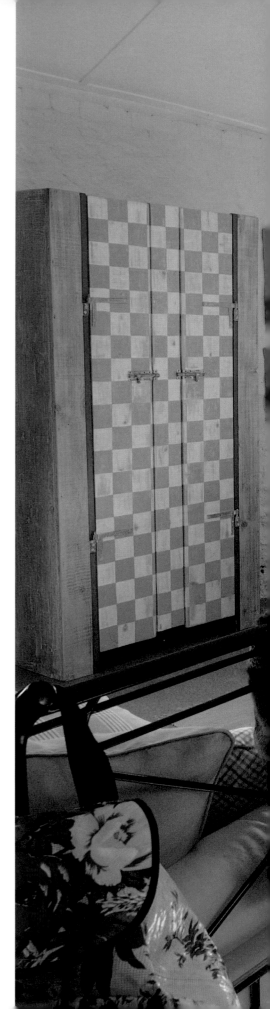

Homely and comfortable, family rooms have a lived-in, easygoing atmosphere in which everyone can gather to chat, relax, and work. They are rooms in which adults can kick off their shoes and wind down, children can spread their homework on the table, and the cat can curl up on the most comfortable chair. Some family rooms are more utilitarian versions of the living room, and others are a cross between a kitchen and living room (sometimes called a "great room"). Many are basically playrooms with a few additions for the adults' comfort, while others are principally work rooms with an area given over to relaxing. Whatever the arrangement, a family room often turns into a jumble of everyone's belongings, with tennis rackets propped up against a pile of library books, a stack of newspapers awaiting someone's attention, and all the other paraphernalia of family living.

Very often, the family room is the last room in the house to be decorated, perhaps because only the family and close friends see it. Yet it does not take much decoration to give a family room new character and style, while still retaining the comfortable atmosphere.

Even though you may decide to throw away some of the clutter, you can still include items that have special meaning to the family, such as a bulletin board covered with favorite family snapshots, or a collection of framed black-and-white or sepia photographs of earlier generations. If the children are still young, you could designate an area of wall as a place to pin up their brightly colored paintings, and use wooden molding to make a frame for a height chart for the children. This makes a decorative feature out of a cherished tradition.

This family room (see also pages 56–57) was converted from an outbuilding into a versatile space where children and parents can work and play together. The bright colors make it an environment for activity rather than relaxation.

FURNISHING PRIORITIES

The number and age of the people who use the room will dictate many of the design decisions, as will the house's other rooms for entertaining. First, as always, you have to assess the space and the existing furniture. Maybe the room lacks a cozy seating area, in the form of a big old armchair or much-loved rocking chair, or perhaps it needs a decorative focal point.

The table will probably be important, especially if the room doubles as a kitchen or dining room, in which case you will need a large, sturdy table. A long refectory style is a good choice, particularly if it has drawers to house placemats, napkins, and the like.

There may not be much room for individual chairs, in which case an old settle, or deacon's bench, would be ideal. What's more, if you choose one with a lid or with a cupboard at the sides (originally used to hang sides of meat) you will have extra storage space. Depending on the condition of the settle, you can either leave the wood bare or give it a distressed paint finish (see page 118) – turquoise blue over deep red looks good, as does forest green over blue.

A collection of attractive cushions on the settle's wooden surface will make it more comfortable as well as providing a pretty combination of patterns.

CREATING ATMOSPHERE

Family rooms are places to feel comfortable and relaxed, so they need to be informal and welcoming. An open log fire or a wood-burning stove is perfect, but if you don't have either of these, you can still create a cozy atmosphere through careful choice of lighting, color, and texture. Colors like cream, deep yellow, russet, dark green, and smoky blue are warm and inviting. Brilliant white, lemon yellow, deep pink, apple green, and chambray blue are appropriate for a cleaner, sunnier, and more contemporary look.

Walls can be painted or wallpapered, but an attractive alternative is to line them with tongue-and-groove paneling, especially if the surface of the walls leaves a lot to be desired. Install it to the height of a chair rail like wainscoting, or to

about 15in (38cm) below the ceiling and surmounted by a narrow shelf – or simply run it from floor to ceiling. It comes in many styles and can be mounted vertically, horizontally, or on the diagonal, then either left natural or painted.

Collections of household objects can be hung on the walls to display their patterns against the plain wall behind – antique trivets, cookie cutters, old-fashioned wooden sieves, carpet beaters, and wicker baskets are all good choices for this treatment.

Look for fabrics with simple patterns for curtains, cushions, and seating, or choose something very colorful for a lively atmosphere. You could even buy a plain linen fabric and paint on your own designs using fabric paint.

LIGHTING

The work area, whether it is used for computing, writing, homework, or craft activities, needs to be well lit, without shadows, while the surrounding areas simply need good overall lighting. You could therefore combine a hanging light or task light such as a gooseneck lamp with several down-lights recessed into the ceiling. Floor lamps or table lamps provide good reading light by sofas or easy chairs. You can also position lights to enhance other features of the room, such as a light to cast shadows over the fireplace or highlight the textures of a wall covering.

PRACTICAL CONSIDERATIONS

Since the family room is one of the most frequently used rooms in the house, it needs to be decorated with a strong emphasis on practicality. Choose curtains in washable cottons, slipcovers that can be removed for cleaning, and flooring that is easily washed or swept. In this room, these practical features are preferable to expensive fabrics that require dry cleaning or a costly carpet that shows every speck of dirt.

Coir and sisal matting are good choices for flooring, unless there are children at the crawling stage. Quarry or brick tiles are another attractive floor covering, but they can be cold underfoot, so vinyl tiles, cork, linoleum – which has completely updated its image – or rubber flooring might be a better choice. A solid floor or floorboards can be covered with wood strip or herringbone-patterned parquet, which gives the room instant warmth and texture. Or existing floorboards can simply be sanded then sealed, painted or stenciled, and finally, varnished.

If you have young children, never display your beautiful china in a family room, and keep breakables out of reach.

A colorful bulletin board is an essential item for keeping important notes and pictures in a busy family room. It is easy to make yourself (see page 60).

CONTEMPORARY WORKROOM

This large, high-ceilinged room, which is shown opposite and also on pages 52–53, was originally an outbuilding but has been converted into a bright, cheerful family room that doubles as a workroom. With its ample work surfaces, storage, and seating, a room like this can be used as a home office or studio by an adult working from home, or by other members of the family for any number of hobbies. A parent can work at one end of the room at the large trestle table desk, while the children sprawl on the pillows at the other end of the room. Or the children can paint or do craft work at the table while a parent keeps a watchful eye from the comfort of the armchair.

Except for the one extravagance – a splendid metal day bed, upholstered in cowslip yellow linen with turquoise piping – virtually all the furnishings are secondhand pieces brightened up with paint. Furnishing with cheap and cheerful items in this way means the whole family can use the workroom to the full without worrying too much about damaging anything.

The room's upbeat, contemporary atmosphere stems partly from the colors themselves – turquoise, cowslip yellow, apple green, and deep pink – and partly from the furniture and the way it has been decorated. The starting point for the whole scheme, and the reason for the distinctly

The informal style of this room makes it a perfect place for children to play or do their homework while parents keep a watchful eye from their worktop or desk.

retro overtones, was the framed collection of textiles from the 1950s which hang on the walls. The curtain fabrics also have a slightly retro feeling because of their bright colors and the splashy, naive-style flowers.

The walls have been deliberately left rough because the uneven surface of the bricks automatically provides character and texture. Painting them turquoise introduces a playful note since it is an unexpected choice for walls like this. In fact, it provides an ideal background for the framed textiles.

Contrasting with the paintwork, the natural colors and textures of the unpainted wooden beams are echoed by those of the simple cork tile flooring. A variety of brightly colored mats and rugs breaks up the floor space with patches of vivid color and pattern.

APPLIQUÉD CUSHIONS

Piles of colorful pillows are irresistible to children. They are perfect for a daybed like the one in our contemporary workroom, providing a comfortable place for children to read or play to their heart's content.

If you need extra seating for an informal room but do not have the space for more chairs, floor pillows are an ideal choice. They also act as padded footstools when you want to relax and stretch out your legs, and are wonderful for children to play on. These floor pillows are easily sewn. One is made from a turquoise and yellow stripe, with yellow piping, and the other from a plain turquoise brushed cotton with pink piping and appliquéd Scottie dogs.

Like everything else in this room, the appliqué is very easy, as the Scotties are cut out of different fabrics and then attached using fusible web. A variety of plain and patterned cottons have been used, all following the room's main color scheme of yellow, apple green, deep pink, and turquoise. The Scottie dogs have been given bows (made from the same ribbons as those used on the bulletin board), adding color and texture to the pillow and creating a three-dimensional effect. It is also a lovely way to bring into the family room an element of design that will appeal to children too.

This idea could be adapted for other images, such as cats, which could be given embroidered whiskers, or rabbits with pompom tails.

PATTERNED THROW

Making a homemade throw insures it will be the right dimensions for your armchair, sofa, or bed. This throw has been made from a piece of heavy, loosely woven Indian cotton, which was chosen for its open-weave texture. For the colorful appliquéd flowers at the corners, vivid shades of orange, pink, apple green, and turquoise have been used. The jazzier and brighter the colors, the more exciting the finished throw will look.

As with all these projects, you can adapt this idea in any way you wish. Choose different images from the flowers, perhaps borrowing the Scottie dogs from the floor cushion, or make a special throw that you bring out each Christmas, using a pattern of Christmas trees or green holly and red berries.

YOU WILL NEED

HEAVY, LOOSELY WOVEN COTTON FABRIC FOR THROW
BRIGHT-COLORED FABRICS FOR APPLIQUÉ
MATCHING SEWING THREAD
CONTRASTING EMBROIDERY FLOSS
COLORED TUBULAR PIPING

1 Cut out the fabric to the correct dimensions, turn under a narrow hem on the edges and hand sew in place using bright embroidery floss; here the idea is for the stitches to show rather than be hidden.

2 For the flower at each corner of the throw, cut petals from colorful fabrics and hand sew them in place using contrasting embroidery floss; as you sew, use your fingers to turn under a narrow hem around the edge of each flower petal.

3 For the center of each flower, coil colored tubular piping in a spiral and hold it in place with a few strategically placed hand stitches.

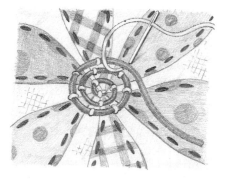

4 Finally, embroider large cross stitches at random all over the throw.

YOU WILL NEED

½IN (1.25CM) THICK CORKBOARD
FELT
STAPLE GUN
RIBBONS
THUMBTACKS

BULLETIN BOARD

If you are working from home, a bulletin board, on which you can keep track of appointments, bills, business cards, press cuttings, fabric samples, photographs, or whatever else you need close at hand, is indispensable. Although you can buy one cheaply, making your own allows you to choose a more interesting color and style in exactly the size you want. The yellow felt backing of this one (also shown on page 55) is the ideal color to place above the desk because it is a jazzy contrast against the turquoise walls. Three types of ribbons have been used – a yellow and turquoise stripe, a turquoise gingham, and an apple green ribbon edged in red.

1 Cut a piece of felt the size of the corkboard plus 2in (5cm) all around. Lay it out on a flat surface and center the corkboard on top.

2 Using the staple gun, staple the felt to the back along all four edges, pulling the felt taut as you do so.

3 Make light marks with a pencil at intervals of about 6in (15cm) all around the edges of the board. The exact distance apart depends on the size of your corkboard, but the marks should be equally spaced.

4 Turn the board over so that it is right side up. Lay one length of ribbon at a time diagonally across the board in one direction, in line with the marks. Staple each one to the back of the board, stretching it taut as you staple the other end, and then move on to the next length of ribbon.

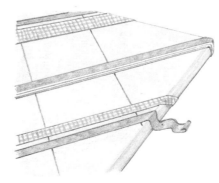

5 Position more lengths of ribbon diagonally the other way, again aligning them with the marks but this time weaving them in and out of the first ribbons. Stretch them taut and staple at the back.

6 Secure the ribbons to the front with thumbtacks around the edges and also in rows at some of the points where the ribbons intersect.

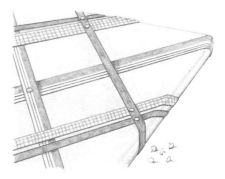

STRIPED BLUEPRINT CHEST

Blueprint chests are principally used by designers and artists, but they are also incredibly useful for household storage. They are ideal for storing children's drawings, large sheets of paper on which children can draw, and old newspapers and magazines they can cut up to make collages. Blueprint chests are also useful for holding catalogs and paperwork, as well as placemats and other table linen.

A blueprint chest is used in this room because it is a workroom as well as a family room, but you could adapt the decorating idea for a large chest of drawers or an old-fashioned, built-in hutch. The idea is extremely simple but very dramatic and is perfect for camouflaging pieces of furniture that have been bought secondhand or are showing their age.

All you need do is take off the handles, remove any previous paint or varnish, sand down the wood, and then paint the blueprint chest in whichever background color you wish. Add the stripes when the final coat of the background color is completely dry. Before you paint them on, measure the width of the area you will be painting, and then calculate how wide each stripe should be for them to fit exactly. It will look best if the stripes at the ends are both in the background color.

Draw faint pencil lines as guide lines and paint the stripes freehand. Or, if you prefer, stick low-tack masking tape along the lines first, to help you paint straight lines, but peel it off very carefully to prevent it from pulling off some of the background paint.

FRAMED TEXTILES

A wonderful alternative to modern pictures or posters in this contemporary family room are the framed large swatches of original 1950s fabrics. Not only might the textiles be valuable one day, but the originality of the designs of these novelty prints makes them lovely framed pieces which look extremely appropriate in this type of setting.

Alternatively, frame remnants of old patchwork quilts or ethnic embroideries and textiles. Swatches of colorful Guatemalan weaves or Indian silks, for example, look exotic framed and grouped together.

PATCHWORK CURTAINS

The playful, upbeat character of this room demanded an unusual window treatment, and these curtains made from panels resembling giant patches create just the right effect. (See the photograph on pages 52–53 for the full curtain.) It is important to keep the panels large because too many small pieces might look rather scattered and could lose their impact. If you have an old pair of lovely time-worn, faded curtains which do not fit the window on which you would like to use them, buying a simple coordinating check or stripe, for example, will enable you to make a whole new set of curtains using this method. Just cut them into large squares or rectangles and join the panels, right sides together, before making them up as lined curtains in the usual way (see pages 68–69).

Choose fabrics with colors and patterns that complement each other – a mixture of checks and contemporary painterly florals has been used here, with apple green, pink, orange, and yellow as the principal colors. Although the fabrics are all different, they have a similar 1950s character and colors, which gives them cohesion.

HARLEQUIN LAMPSHADE

Here is a quick way to brighten up a plain paper lampshade. All you need are some artist's oil pastels in suitable colors, such as the red, pink, lime, yellow, black, blue, and orange used here. The stripes are drawn freehand, so practice on some paper before beginning work on the lampshade itself. The stripes are thicker at the bottom of the lampshade, tapering almost to points at the top to echo the lampshade's basic conical shape. If you look closely, you will see that the texture of the paper has been allowed to show through quite clearly, for a pleasing, spontaneous character.

There is no need to spray the oil pastels with fixative, but if you use chalk instead you should.

The lamp base is a simple, modern, painted column, with the beading painted in yellow. If you buy a base from a secondhand shop, you may be able to paint each section a different color, or add painted stripes or circles.

CHECKERED CUPBOARD

The wooden cupboard in the photograph on pages 52–53 has been painted to emphasize its pair of central doors. The sides of the cupboard were roughly painted in shades of green, and then, when dry, some of the paint was rubbed back to allow the grain and texture of the wood to come through. The doors and central panel have been painted in green and cream checks.

HARVEST FAMILY ROOM

This family room was decorated with a harvest theme clearly visible in the combination of golden yellow, yellow ocher, and warm reds and greens, and in the Provençal fabric. The botanical prints on the walls, depicting a range of fruit as well as flowers, continue the harvest theme, providing such a rich tapestry of color and pattern that the rest of the room requires little decoration. They create a stunning alternative to wallpaper or paint in this warm, autumnal family room.

The wooden beams of the ceiling have been painted cream and, in one corner, hung with bunches of drying flowers waiting to be turned into potpourri and dried arrangements.

The Provençal-patterned curtains have deliberately been kept simple. Hung from wooden curtain poles, they fit in well with the rustic atmosphere of the room and enhance rather than overwhelm the botanical prints. The integral valances, reminiscent of a dirndl skirt, add visual appeal and are echoed by the pleated skirts on the seat covers.

Botanical prints taken from an old Laura Ashley calendar provide an usual alternative to wallpaper in this cozy family room where the decorating scheme is based around fall colors and motifs.

BOTANICAL PRINTS

If you want to decorate a wall without using wallpaper, create your own montage of special prints or drawings. In this room, twelve botanical prints from an old calendar have been chosen to fit in with the harvest theme of the room, but there are many other patterns to choose from. As a starting point, create a montage of attractive images with pictures from a current calendar, illustrations from a poster book, or a collection of notecards or postcards. For a graphic look, use sheet music, pages taken from newspapers, or reproductions of architectural drawings. Whatever the effect you want to create, choose images that are striking, blend together, and look good from a distance.

Once you have chosen the images, you need to have them photocopied onto large sheets of

paper – we used 11 x 17in (28 x 43cm) paper. The botanical prints in this room were color-copied onto cream paper to make them look antique, but you could use regular photocopies when reproducing monochrome prints or black and white photographs. These photocopies were pasted onto the wall in simple rows using wallpaper paste, with their edges butting up to one another, but they could be placed in a more random arrangement. If you are unsure about which pictures to group together, position them on the floor first so you can see which colors and shapes go well together. For instance, if you are using botanical prints, you might want to place a picture of oranges next to one of daffodils for a pleasing contrast.

Once the photocopies are pasted onto the wall a coat of varnish should be applied to protect them. Flat polyurethane varnish was used for these prints but a lightly tinted varnish could be used instead if you want to make the prints look attractively aged.

In this room, the lower portion of the wall has been painted, and then the botanical prints have been pasted above the painted area. This not only protects them from scuffs but also prevents them from overpowering the room, which they would if used from ceiling to floor on every wall. An alternative might be to cover an alcove completely in prints, leaving the rest of the room plain, or to cover only one wall from floor to ceiling. The same prints could also be used to make a decoupage object, such as a screen, trunk, tabletop, or tray.

CURTAINS WITH INTEGRAL VALANCES

Curtains in a family room like this look best when kept relatively simple. Anything fussy is too formal for this comfortable, relaxing space. However, simple does not have to mean boring, as proved by these pretty curtains.

Curtains with integral valances are an interesting twist on a classic form. They are particularly suitable for rooms that need all the daylight they can get because the valance moves

with the curtain and can be opened. They look attractive whatever the dimensions of the window and are suitable for wooden, brass, or wrought-iron curtain poles.

The curtains in this room were lined using the sewn-in lining method, but the valances were left unlined. Instead of using only one fabric you could give the valances a border of another fabric, perhaps one that is used elsewhere in the room for the upholstery of an armchair or for some pillows, or a contrasting plain fabric.

Narrow valances will look wrong unless the curtains themselves are very short. The exact depth of the valance will be determined by the length of the curtains and, possibly, the weight of the curtain fabric. Professionals usually recommend that they be at least one-sixth to one-fifth the length of the curtains.

MEASURING

For the length of each curtain, measure from the pole or rod to the desired length, and add ½in (1.25cm) for the upper seam allowance and 5in (12.5cm) for the lower hem. The width of each curtain should be the full length of the pole or rod plus 3in (7.5cm) for the two side hems. (With two curtains, this will give you a fullness of double the finished width, which is suitable for shirred and pinch-pleated self-styling curtain tapes.)

Your lining should be the same length as the curtains, and it should be the same width as the curtains less 2in (5cm) for each curtain.

Each integral valance should be the desired length (see above) plus 2in (5cm), and the same width as each curtain. They are not lined.

YOU WILL NEED

FABRIC FOR CURTAIN AND INTEGRAL VALANCE
LINING FABRIC
MATCHING SEWING THREAD
SELF-STYLING TAPE AND HOOKS
LEAD CURTAIN WEIGHTS (OPTIONAL)
CURTAIN POLE AND RINGS, OR ROD

1 Cut out the curtains, joining fabric widths if necessary; do the same for the integral valance and the lining.

2 With right sides together, pin the curtain to the lining at each side edge, trimming the bottom edge of the lining so it is ¾in (2cm) above the bottom (raw) edge of the curtain. Stitch a ½in (1.25cm) seam on each side, stopping 10in (25.5cm) from the lower edge of the curtain.

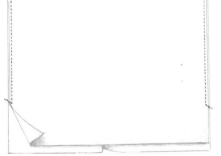

3 Turn right side out and press, forming a 1in (2.5cm) hem along each side. Press under the seam allowances on the unstitched sides.

4 Turn under and press ½in (1.25cm) and then 1in (2.5cm) on both side edges and the lower edge of the integral valance, mitering the lower corners as shown. Stitch.

5 Place the valance on the back of the curtain, with the right side of the valance facing the right side of the lining, and the top and side edges even. Stitch a ½in (1.25cm) seam across the top. Press the seam open.

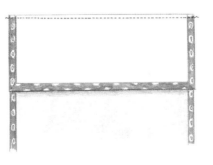

6 Turn the valance to the curtain front along the seamline; baste in place.

7 The distance from the top edge of the curtain to the top of the self-styling tape will depend on your curtain pole and rings (or rod) and your tape.

Position the tape over the lining. Knot the two cords together on the leading (center) edge of the curtain and turn under ¼in (6mm) at the end of the tape. Pin and then stitch across the end and along both edges, through the tape, lining, curtain, and valance, stitching in the same direction each time. At the outside edge, turn under the end and stitch across it, keeping the cords free. Remove the basting.

8 Turn up ¼in (6mm) and then 3in (7.5cm) on the lower edge of both the curtain and the lining. At each corner, fold the corner of the lower edge in at an angle to resemble a miter, as shown. Hand sew the curtain hem, and machine stitch the lining hem, inserting weights in the curtain hem if desired.

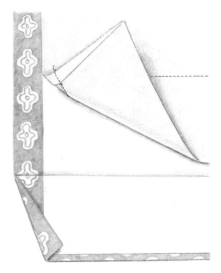

9 Pull the cords on the tape to form gathers or pleats. When the curtain is the correct width, knot the cords together. (Do not cut them off.) Insert hooks, and hang from the rings on the pole or from the rod.

LINED CAT BASKET

Any self-respecting cat is extremely choosy about where it sleeps. Some cats delight in going to sleep on the very piece of fabric, newspaper, or armchair that you were about to use, while others head straight for the warmest area in the house. This attractive and comfortable basket, however, makes all other sleeping places pale in comparison.

As the lined basket will be a permanent part of the furnishings, you should see that it fits into the room's decorating scheme. The cat basket shown here is a pleasing combination of pattern and texture, and both the wicker exterior and the Provençal fabric interior match the rustic, informal style of the room.

The basket lining, which is machine-washable, may be made to fit a larger basket and then used for a dog basket.

MEASURING

Make a pattern using brown paper or newspaper. Inside the basket, cover the base with paper, creasing it around the sides; trim to shape. Cut out two pieces of fabric and one of batting, adding ½in (1.25cm) all around.

With the base pattern in place inside the basket, make a pattern for the rim, cutting a strip to fit all the way around the rim and across the entrance, starting and stopping at center front. If the rim of the basket slopes, cut slits in the strip at regular intervals, from the top almost to the bottom so that each slit opens up to fit the sloping rim. Fill in the triangular spaces with small pieces of paper, securing them in place with sticky tape. Mark the entrance on the pattern, and draw a line ½in (1.25cm) above this; cut along that line.

Use this pattern to cut two fabric pieces on the bias for the rim, adding ½in (1.25cm) to each end and cutting away this amount from the top edge, except for the entrance (where you should cut along the pattern).

Cut pieces of batting, and baste them together to make a strip the same size as the rim pieces.

For the ruffle, measure from one side of the entrance, around the basket, to the other side of the entrance. From the same fabric, cut a 4in (10cm) wide strip approximately twice as long as this distance.

1 For the ruffle, fold the long strip in half lengthwise, right sides together, and stitch a narrow seam across each end. Turn right side out, fold in half lengthwise with wrong sides together, and press. Form the ruffle into regularly spaced knife pleats – ours are ⅜in (1cm) wide and 1¼in (3cm) apart. Adjust the pleats until the pleated ruffle fits around one rim piece, stopping ½in (1.25cm) short of the entrance on each side. Baste the ruffle to hold the pleats in place.

2 Baste the batting to the wrong side of one rim piece. With raw edges even, baste the ruffle to the right side of this

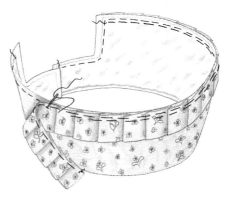

piece along the top, starting and stopping ½in (1.25cm) before the entrance edges.

3 With right sides together, join the ends of one strip with a ½in (1.25cm) seam. Repeat for the other strip so you have two rings. Press the seams and turn one ring right side out. Matching the center front seams, put one ring inside the other so the right sides are together and raw edges even.

4 With the right sides together, join the rings around the top with a ½in (1.25cm) seam. Trim the seam. Clip into the curves within the seam allowance. Turn right side out, and press.

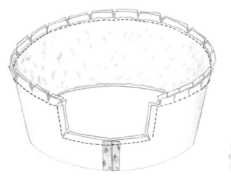

5 Place the two base fabric pieces with wrong sides together, and slip the base batting piece between them. Baste ½in (1.25cm) from the edge all around.

6 With right sides together and raw edges even, join the inner rim piece to the base, taking a ½in (1.25cm) seam.

Clip curves, and trim away the seam allowance of the base batting.

7 Trim off ½in (1.25cm) from the lower edge of the rim batting. Turn under this amount along the outer rim piece and slipstitch along the seamline all around the edge on the bottom of the base. Remove any visible basting.

PAINTED MEAT SAFE

In the days before refrigerators, food was stored in a variety of places including pantries (which were built onto an outside wall of the house, preferably a north-facing wall, to insure the pantry stayed cool) and meat safes. Today, meat safes are prized more for their decorative appearance than their food-keeping qualities, and they are generally used to house everything and anything but food. They can be filled with a precious collection of antique pitchers, or old baking ware, soup tureens, and vegetable dishes – even toy cars and folk art wooden animals that are close to your heart.

Originally, for ventilation purposes, many meat safes had doors with insets of punched metal in which the holes formed various patterns, and these still look marvelous. Others, like the one shown in the photograph opposite, had chicken wire or glazed doors so that the contents were easily visible, and it is these meat safes that are so useful as small display cabinets.

You can paint a meat safe in any way you wish. Give it a contemporary appearance with fresh coats of paint in bright and sophisticated colors, or paint it a simple background color and then decorate it with stencils or stamping (see pages 114–115 and page 51 respectively). Other possibilities include leaving it in its original state, or creating your own antiqued look (see pages 118–119) using the room's predominant colors.

SEAT COVERS WITH SKIRTS

Even the most attractive wooden chair can become uncomfortable without a padded seat cover. Several styles of seat covers are shown in this book, varying with the shape of the chair. To make the covers shown here, follow the directions given on pages 42–45, using your chosen fabric and including an extra skirt piece between the struts.

These seat covers were made from the same Provençal cotton as the curtains, with pleated skirts in a coordinating striped cotton printed with berries and olives. Two self-ties at the back of the seat cover anchor it to the chair.

Combining pattern in this way is ideal for a relaxed, country-style room although the basic shape of the seat covers would work just as well in an elegant dining room if you used an appropriate fabric. They will also look more formal with one fabric for the seat cover and skirt and a contrasting material for the piping. Alternatively, if the chair legs are straight, you could make a cover with a floor-length skirt.

JAM JAR COVERS

There is something very satisfying about seeing jars of homemade preserves topped with colorful circles of fabric. These fabric tops make the contents of the jars look all the more enticing, emphasizing that they are home-produced.

Jam jar covers are easy to make and are the ideal finishing touch if you are giving some of your own homemade preserves as a gift. Keep some for yourself too – they look marvelous arranged on a shelf or in a glass-fronted cupboard. Group them with an eye to their colors and textures: a row of jewel-colored jams can look quite dazzling. (You can, of course, cheat and decorate the jam jars whether you made their contents or not!)

A selection of fruit prints was used for these jam jar covers to tie in with the harvest theme, but traditional gingham, or stripes, or even denim can be used instead. You might also choose patterns that reflect the contents of the jars, such as a berry pattern for raspberry, strawberry, or blackberry jam, a cherry design for brandied cherries, or a vegetable print for pickles and chutneys.

YOU WILL NEED

Assorted fabrics

Matching or contrasting sewing thread

½in (1.25cm) wide bias binding

¼in (6mm) wide elastic

Twine

Pinking shears (optional)

1 For a single elasticized square, cut a piece of fabric about 8in (20.5cm) square (or larger or smaller according to the size of the jar) and turn under ¼in (6mm) on each edge; stitch. On the wrong side, draw a circle large enough to wrap over the jar lid. Pin bias binding around the circle on the wrong side, and stitch along both edges. Attach a safety pin to elastic and thread it through the casing. Cut the elastic a little shorter than the distance around the circle. Hand sew the ends of the elastic together, and

the ends of the bias tape together to close the opening.

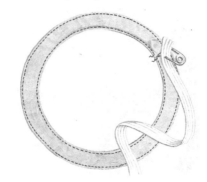

2 For a double elasticized square, cut two 8in (20.5cm) squares and hem the edges of each, as in step 1. Place them together, right sides facing up, as shown, and baste together. Treat the squares as one layer, and proceed as for step 1. Remove basting.

3 For an elasticized circle, cut an 8in (20.5cm) circle and turn under ¼in (6mm) all around the edge. Stitch, then proceed as for step 1.

4 For an elasticized scalloped cover, make a pattern by cutting a circle and scalloping the edge. Use the pattern to cut out one fabric piece, then turn the pattern over to cut out another, from a different fabric. Matching scallops, place the pieces with right sides together. Stitch a narrow seam all around, leaving an opening. Clip curves, and turn right side out. Slipstitch the opening and press. Elasticize as for step 1.

5 For a tied circle, cut a circle as for step 3, but just tie it with twine. Instead of hemming the edges, you could cut it out with pinking shears.

PROVENÇAL CUSHIONS

The deacon's bench in this room looks particularly inviting with its array of brightly colored pillows making a fine contrast against the rich, dark tones of the wood. Of the five different fabric patterns, two do not appear anywhere else in the room yet their floral and fruit motifs and colors insure they fit in well with the overall theme of warm autumn colors and a bountiful harvest. Because of their similar tones and small-scale pattern, the different fabrics on the pillows go well together and add to the warm, cozy atmosphere of the room. The same fabrics are used on the jars of preserves (see page 74 for how to make these covers), helping to link the whole scheme together.

With so much color and pattern, all that is needed on the pillows is simple self-piping. To make the pillow covers, just join two fabric squares together around the edges, inserting piping into the seams as directed on page 44, steps 6, 7, and 8. Either leave an opening in one side (inserting a zipper or slipstitching it closed) or create an opening in the back by substituting for the square two overlapping rectangles on which the overlapping edges are hemmed.

CHAPTER FIVE

Kitchens

The kitchen is the hub, the nerve-center, and the heart of the house. It is where children congregate after school to delve into cookie jars, where dogs and cats curl up in front of the warm stove, and where a family might gather together with hot mugs of coffee after a wet and windy country walk.

What your kitchen says about you would probably keep a psychologist busy for years. Is it a tribute to the gleaming qualities of stainless steel or the warm, homely feel of wood? Have you kept the room as streamlined as possible or is it a testament to your passion for collecting everything from antique cookie cutters to teapots? Any of these things will say a lot about you and will add a particular character to the room.

Because the kitchen is the hub of the household, most people want it to look comfortable and inviting. A wood-burning stove provides a wonderful focal point, but people will also gravitate to a cozy corner with a table and a couple of comfortable chairs.

The unfitted kitchen with its freestanding furniture creates more of a countrified atmosphere than fitted cabinets, but it needs to be planned carefully if it is to be functional. Include as much counter area as possible, then create storage space with a hutch, open shelves, an old wall-hung cupboard or two, and possibly a chest of drawers or armoire.

The hutch in the seaside kitchen (see pages 82–83) is laden with simple blue and white earthenware. Its informality and fresh color make it appropriate for a seaside setting. The blue and white stripes of the collection could have provided the starting point for the decorating scheme instead of the seaside theme.

PRACTICAL CONSIDERATIONS

The kitchen is usually the most practical room in the house, so it has to be decorated accordingly. Before you start to plan your decorations, you need to think of the main structure – the appliances such as the refrigerator, the stove or oven and cooktop, the counters, and the sink. Unless you are redesigning your entire kitchen, you will have to choose a decorative scheme that complements that structure.

In high-tech, streamlined kitchens, hard textures and surfaces predominate. Soft textures – curtains, tea towels, upholstered seating, and tablecloths – would look out of place in such a spare environment but would look very much at home in cozy, more countrified kitchens with a lot of wood.

Selecting the right flooring is particularly important in kitchens because you need a surface that is practical and can be easily cleaned

yet is in keeping with the decorative scheme. Waxed, varnished, or painted wooden floorboards are always attractive, and can be placed under a kitchen table, making for a cozy end of the room. Other options include vinyl and linoleum, both of which come in sheet and also tile form, and quarry or ceramic tiles.

Available in almost every size, shape, color, and design imaginable, ceramic tiles can also be used on counters and backsplashes, and they provide instant texture. Arranging the tiles in inventive patterns helps to make them look more interesting – rectangular tiles can be laid in herringbone patterns, square tiles can be laid on their points so they look like diamonds, or you can combine the two shapes for a basketweave effect. You can also experiment with color, perhaps using alternate tiles in different shades of the same color, or combining tiles in colors from the same part of the spectrum or arranging black tiles around the edge so that they form a border for the white tiles within.

Sometimes the simplest approaches are the most successful. The uneven edges, subtle colors, and lovely textures of thick, hand-made tiles, for example, are so attractive in themselves that pattern is often superfluous.

If you wish to use wallpaper, choose one that is washable, particularly if you have a small

A simple floral sprig wallpaper in sapphire blue makes a lovely, fresh wall covering for this country kitchen. The sapphire blue is picked out for the painted woodwork and is complemented by the pretty yellow tablecloth.

kitchen in which steam can be a problem. You may prefer to use paint, in which case washability is again an important factor. Latex velvet (which is water-based but washable and hard-wearing) is ideal for kitchen walls, while eggshell (a hard-wearing, washable, oil-based paint with a sheen rather than a gloss) is excellent for doors, baseboards, and other woodwork.

INTRODUCING TEXTURE AND PATTERN

There are many ways to add interesting texture and pattern to the kitchen. If there is space for a table and chairs, you can give these various treatments according to the overall style of the room. If the table is wooden and has seen better days, rub it down with fine steel wool or very fine sandpaper, apply a little polish, and buff it hard to get a long-lasting, silky sheen. Alternatively, paint it in a solid color, distressing it if you wish. Don't forget that a gaily patterned tablecloth will hide a multitude of sins. The chairs may look good in their natural state, or you can paint them and give them attractive padded cushions, or make full-length slipcovers for them (see pages 132–133).

If the cabinet doors are dreary or unattractive you may be able to fit new doors to the existing cabinets. If not, you can paint the doors, then decorate them with stamping, stenciling, or decoupage (see pages 51, 114, and 28 respectively). Each of these treatments can be protected with several coats of flat varnish. Another possibility is to take off the cabinet doors and put up simple cotton panels gathered onto thin curtain wire.

Glass-fronted cabinets are useful because they allow the colors and patterns of the contents to show while at the same time keeping them clean.

You can add further interest with a strip of filet lace along the front.

An old-fashioned rise-and-fall overhead airer looks pretty in a cottage-style or farmhouse kitchen bedecked with linen tea towels and drying herbs and flowers.

Displays of kitchen equipment, books, and china also provide instant color and pattern. Hang ropes of garlic, and strings of drying red chillies from the ceiling. Attractive cookie jars, olive oil cans, bottles of vinegar, and cans of olives all look superb on display.

There is more opportunity for using hard textures – for example, the collection of enamelware in the blue and and white kitchen (see page 91) or a hutch bursting with a collection of colonial slipware. To really jazz up a scheme in what is essentially the most practical room in the house, opt for bolder patterns or choose a theme like hens to collect or a seaside theme, which was appropriate for the kitchen shown overleaf and on pages 78–79.

Window treatments must be practical in the kitchen. Roller shades or Venetian blinds (which are available with natural or stained wood slats as well as the familiar metal type), colonial style slatted shutters, or simple café curtains are all functional options that look good too.

BLUE AND WHITE KITCHEN

This cheerful, summery kitchen has a relaxed and comfortable atmosphere that is a million miles away from the sophistication of a gleaming, fitted kitchen. Instead, its informal, seaside look has been inspired by the beach which lies a few yards away. It is a room in which the family can gather to eat, relax, read, and prepare picnics to eat on the beach. The French windows lead out onto a timber deck that overlooks the sea and is the ideal place to eat breakfasts and relaxed brunches in the summer. Because this is a weekend retreat and vacation home, the scheme is kept simple and quite practical. The kitchen end of the room is the ultimate in simplicity, with a small stove, a sink and fridge, and a cupboard.

The starting point of this scheme was the beautiful washed blue muslin with cornflowers used for the curtains. The colors evoke the blue sea and high, puffy summer clouds of the seashore, and blue and white is a classic combination for a kitchen.

In this room, the main patterns are stripes and checks, with the pottery on the dresser adding more stripes. Even the white-painted paneling on the walls and ceilings is a seaside building material and adds to the informality of the room. A practical, plastic rug of blue, white, and black

On a summer's day, when the windows are flung open onto the deck with the beach and blue sea beyond, this room, with its whitewashed tongue-and-groove walls and fresh chambray blue color, becomes an extension of the seaside.

stripes provides a splash of color on the bleached wooden floorboards. Chambray blue linen shades at the French windows help to keep out chilly sea breezes and create another big splash of blue. Hand-painted tiles behind the sink continue the blue and white checked theme.

The furniture is simple, consisting of a white painted woven-fiber chair, with white-painted benches and an upright kitchen chair at the table. The woven-fiber chair has actually been given three alternative treatments to show just what is possible: an upholstered seat, a slipcover for summer made from towels, and a slipcover for winter made from cream blankets.

HAND-PAINTED TILES

If you can't find any tiles that you really like for your kitchen, or you want something unique, try painting your own tiles with ceramic paints. They cannot be used in areas that will need a lot of cleaning, because the paint will eventually rub off. However, the beauty of hand-painted tiles is that they are not meant to look perfect, so there is no need to worry about producing designs that are mathematically exact. Paint your designs freehand, choosing a motif that echoes an element of the room's decorating scheme. Instead of checks, you could create other patterns such as diamonds, flowers, leaves, fruits, or berries. Good-quality brushes are essential for painting tiles well, so choose yours carefully.

YOU WILL NEED

TILES (ALREADY IN PLACE)
CERAMIC PAINTS IN DARK BLUE AND WHITE
ROUND ARTIST'S FITCH BRUSH
1IN (2.5CM) WIDE FLAT DECORATOR'S BRUSH

1 Make sure your tiles are very clean. From a piece of paper or cardboard, cut a square the size of a tile, and cut a tiny hole at the center point. Use this template to lightly mark the center of each tile, with either a pencil or colored chalk.

2 Using the flat brush and dark blue paint, paint 1in (2.5cm) wide vertical and horizontal bands through the center of each tile to the edges. The roughness is part of the look, so you shouldn't need to use a ruler unless you want the effect much neater.

3 When dry, paint over the blue bands with a diluted white paint to make it look a little softer.

4 Mix some white into the dark blue to make a lighter blue, and paint the narrow stripes on each side of the band using the round brush.

Muslin fabric with stripes about
3¼in (8.5cm) wide and spaced about
5½in (14cm) apart
Matching sewing thread
Lightweight fusible interfacing
Mother-of-pearl buttons
Curtain weights (optional)

MEASURING

For the length, measure from about
1½in (4cm) below the pole to the floor.
Cut the fabric to this measurement
plus 4½in (11.5cm) for the top turning
and a further 8in (20.5cm) for the
lower hem.

For the width, measure the pole,
multiply the measurement by about
one and a half, and add 2in (5cm) for
each side hem.

Vary the size of the tabs to suit your
fabric and the thickness of your pole.
Ours were each made from two
3¼ x 14in (8.5 x 35.5cm) strips cut
from the striped portion of the fabric
and using the full width of the stripe.

MUSLIN CURTAINS WITH BUTTONED TABS

These simple, unlined curtains were the starting point for the whole
design. They are made from a muslin fabric featuring chambray blue
washed stripes alternated with a botanical print of lilies of the valley,
cornflowers, and bees. They have a clean, fresh look that is ideal for
this kitchen, and the sheer fabric filters the sunlight that streams into
the room. Blue linen shades also hang at the window and the light
shining through reveals the texture of the linen.

Furthering the seaside theme of the kitchen, starfish were attached
using wood glue to the ends of the narrow, white-painted curtain
pole to act as finials. They are permanent fixtures, so the curtains are
removed for washing by unbuttoning the tabs that are looped over
the pole. The shell-like mother-of-pearl buttons on the tabs also echo
the seashore locale.

The tabs are cut from the blue part of the fabric and positioned so
that the blue stripes in the curtain seem to extend over the back of
the pole and button at the front.

1 Cut out the curtains and join the
fabric widths if necessary. Press under
a double 1in (2.5cm) hem on each side
of the curtains; stitch.

2 Following the manufacturer's
directions, iron on a 3in (7.5cm) wide
strip of fusible interfacing ½in
(1.25cm) away from the top edge of
each curtain. Fold the seam allowance
over the interfacing. Now fold the
fabric along the bottom edge of the

interfacing. Press and baste along both
folded edges and across the ends.

3 To make each tab, place the two
strips with right sides together, and
stitch a ¼in (6mm) seam down each
long side, tapering the stitching to a
point at one end. Trim across the point
and the corners, then turn right side
out and press. Make a buttonhole at
the end of each tab, just before the tab
begins to narrow.

4 Position the tabs on the back of the curtain in line with the stripes, and pointing downward, with the raw end ¾in (2cm) above the lower folded edge. Pin, then check that the tabs will be the correct length when wrapped over the pole and buttoned; adjust if necessary. Baste in place. Stitch along this edge from one side of the curtain to the other, stitching over the tabs.

5 Fold the tabs up toward the top, covering the raw edges. Press and baste near the top edge. Stitch across one end of the heading, then along the top edge (stitching through the tabs as well) and finally across the other end.

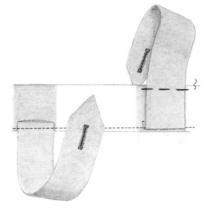

6 For each tab, sew a button to the curtain. Stitch across the tab (only) above the buttonhole in line with the upper row of stitching on the curtain top. Remove all basting, and button the curtains onto the pole.

7 Turn up a double 4in (10cm) deep hem on the lower edge, checking the length with the curtains in position. (There is no need to miter the corners on sheer curtains.) Add curtain weights at the corners if desired, then press and hand sew the hem in place.

SIMPLE CHAIR COVER

Even an old woven-fiber or wicker chair that has seen better days can be transformed with fabric. If necessary, paint the chair first with two or three coats of latex. It is an easy, although time-consuming job – just make sure you get the paint into all the crevices. (This procedure is best done outdoors because the paint can spatter in all directions if you are not careful.)

YOU WILL NEED

Upholstery fleece (optional)
Fabric
Upholstery tacks

1 Decide whether you will need to add any padding to the seat. If extra padding is needed, fold up plenty of fleece into roughly the required shape, then trim one side into a curve and place it on the chair seat.

2 Cut out a piece of fabric large enough to fit over the chair seat and extend down over the front, then tuck the raw edges under around the sides of the seat and secure them in place by hammering in upholstery tacks.

3 Stretch the fabric down over the front and tack. Turn the chair upside down and tack the final edge in place.

SUMMER CHAIR SLIPCOVER

A terrycloth slipcover like this is ideal for a beach house or the sitting area beside a swimming pool because it is practical and hard-wearing, will act like a towel, and can easily be removed for washing. This cover was made from two large beach towels stitched together. The finished edges of the towels were utilized as much as possible, which meant that many seams could be made simply by overlapping edges, and a hem on the lower edge was unnecessary. Terrycloth purchased by the yard could be used instead, but you would have to hem and seam the edges in the conventional way.

YOU WILL NEED

2 IDENTICAL BEACH TOWELS, AT LEAST 3 X 5FT (90 X 150CM)
MATCHING SEWING THREAD

1 Place one of the towels in the chair so that it covers the back both inside and outside the chair. Make vertical darts wherever necessary to shape it to the back. It's easiest to do this with the towel wrong side up, so you can pin the darts on the outside. Baste the darts.

2 Cut a strip along the edge of the other towel, long enough to wrap right around the lower portion of the chair. Cut the remainder of this towel into a piece to cover the seat (positioned so the finished edge is at the front) and a piece for each side.

3 Where the two sides meet the back, overlap the edges so that the finished edge will be on top when the cover is turned right side out; baste. (If the finished edge does not run along this portion, baste the two raw edges with right sides together.)

4 With all the pieces wrong side up, baste the piece covering the seat to the bottom of the inner back piece, with right sides together.

5 With right sides together, baste the outer side to the inner side over the arm, and baste it to the side of the seat cover beneath that. Repeat for the other arm.

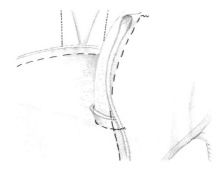

6 Baste the strip going around the bottom to the front edge of the seat and to the lower edge of the sides and outer back. The finished edge of the bottom strip will run along the bottom. The finished edges of the seat front and of the sides and back should be on top when turned right side out.

7 Turn the cover right side out and check that it fits. Often chairs like this are not exactly symmetrical, so you may have to make slight adjustments. Trim away any excess fabric.

8 Finally, turn wrong side out and stitch all the seams. Trim seams, clip curves, and remove basting.

WINTER CHAIR SLIPCOVER

This snug, cozy slipcover is ideal for the winter because it has been made from two old cream-colored blankets. Woven-fiber chairs, like wicker chairs, can be rather chilly and uncomfortable on their own, but this soft slipcover insures warmth and comfort. Its construction is much the same as the terrycloth cover, but if you use a large blanket, there will be fewer seams.

The edges of the blanket have been used to make the skirt of the slipcover, to avoid the need for hemming and to retain the decorative blanket stitch trimming. The two front seams joining the arms together have been oversewn with blanket stitch using blue yarn. Patches of tartan have been sewn onto the slipcover at random, using large overcasting stitches. Before sewing, turn under the raw edges of the tartan to prevent them from raveling. If you prefer, you can sew on patches of felt (which does not need to be turned under), or you can cut out the patches using pinking shears to reduce the amount of raveling and produce an interesting finish.

YOU WILL NEED

1 OR 2 OLD BLANKETS
CONTRASTING COTTON FABRIC FOR PATCHES
MATCHING SEWING THREAD
CONTRASTING YARN

1 Make up the cover as for the summer cover, using one or two old blankets instead of beach towels. If you are using just one blanket, you will not be able to position a finished edge in so many places as with the two towels, so the unfinished edges should be joined with right sides together.

2 Blanket stitch the front edges using contrasting yarn.

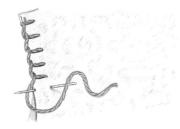

3 Cut out rectangular patches from cotton fabric, turn under a narrow hem on each raw edges and hand sew the patches at random to the cover using the contrasting yarn.

GINGHAM CUSHIONS

You can produce very easy, informal seating by making a box cushion for a long bench, as directed for the cushions on the window seats on pages 108–109, omitting the buttoning. This cushion has been covered with blue and white gingham edged with self-piping. In keeping with the seaside theme, the cushion is held in place with white rope, threaded through eyelets and tied underneath the bench. Simply stitch three small flaps into the seam on each long edge on the underside of the cushion, and punch the eyelets in them.

The wooden chair that is used at the end of the table in this kitchen has been given a simple, self-piped seat pad in blue and white gingham, which matches the bench cushion. Instead of ties, the seat pad is held in place with rope knotted around the chair back and threaded through eyelets, punched in the two back corners of the seat pad.

For both the box cushion and the chair seat pad, the white rope we used had a blue thread running through it, which was ideal for the blue gingham cushions.

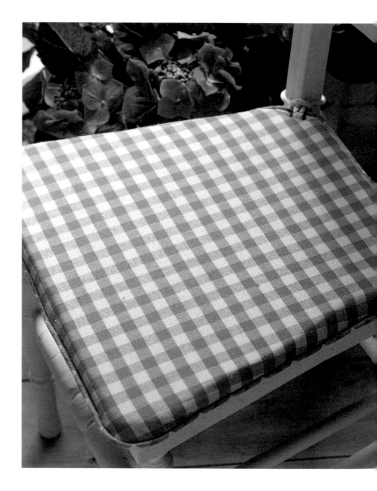

PAINTED ENAMELWARE

Old enamel jugs and buckets can be given a new lease on life with paint, and their simple shapes make them easy and satisfying to decorate. The two pitchers shown here continue the theme of checks, and seaside motifs have been stenciled in white. The small cooking pot has been painted with a spattered effect, while the large bucket has been spray-painted with gradations of color from a blue top to a white bottom.

Pitchers, pots, and buckets like these can often be found in secondhand shops and can also be bought new. Enamel plates and mugs could be decorated in the same way. Although you would not be able to eat from them, they would look very good arranged on the shelves of a hutch.

When you are working with spray paints, always protect the surrounding area with newspaper, as they are messy. Work in a well ventilated room (or outdoors) and wear a paper mask for protection against the fumes.

YOU WILL NEED

Clear super enamel spray paint such as Plasti-Kote

For pitchers
Enamel pitcher
Spray paints in dark blue, light blue, green, cream, and white
Model-making enamel paint in white
Low-tack masking tape
Shell motif stencil
Stencil brush

For cooking pot
Enamel cooking pot
Oil paints in 2 or 3 colors
Mineral spirits
Short-bristled brush such as stencil brush or old toothbrush, or long-haired decorator's brush and stick

For bucket
Spray paints in medium blue, light blue, and white

Enamel pitchers

1 Remove any flaking or rusty areas using fine sandpaper, then spray with clear super enamel spray paint.

2 Use low-tack masking tape to mask out the areas that will not be sprayed with your first color. Spray the remaining blocks with that color. When dry, remove the tape carefully, remask, and spray the second color.

Continue till all the blocks are sprayed. Spray the handle too.

3 Buy or cut your own shell motif stencil, and stencil the shells onto some of the blocks using white enamel paint (undiluted).

Enamel cooking pot

1 Prepare the surface as for the enamel pitchers, step 1.

2 Dilute the oil paint with mineral spirits until it is the consistency of milk. If, when you begin spattering, the spots are too big, your paint may need to be diluted a little more. Take up a little of one color on your brush and hold the brush above the can. Avoid holding it too close to the can.

3 If you are using a short-bristled brush, hold the brush upside down and run your finger or a knife blade over the bristles to spatter tiny specks of color onto the billycan.

4 If you are using a long-haired brush, either tap the brush with the stick or tap the stick with the brush, spattering specks of paint onto the surface.

5 Spatter the whole surface. When dry, add a second layer if desired.

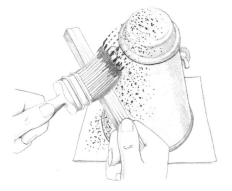

Enamel bucket

1 Prepare the surface as for the enamel pitchers, step 1.

2 Using the medium blue paint, spray the top half of the bucket, fading it out to nothing as you work downward.

3 Using the light blue paint, continue spraying the color, gradually fading it away as you get nearer the bottom of the bucket.

4 Turn the bucket upside down. Starting at the bottom of the bucket, spray with white, gradually fading the color away as you work toward the top of the bucket.

APPLIQUÉ NAPKINS

Continuing the seaside theme, the blue linen napkins shown on the right have been decorated with appliquéd shell motifs. The motifs have been cut out of the same fabric as the shell tablecloth (see pages 94–95), then the edges of the motifs have been turned under and hand-sewn in place.

APPLIQUÉ TABLECLOTHS

Two very different tablecloths appear in this kitchen. The first, shown on the kitchen table, has been interlined so that it can be used not only as a tablecloth but also as a sofa throw and picnic rug. The plain blue linen forms the basis of the tablecloth and the gingham strips are stitched on top of the linen. The tablecloth is reversible, with blue gingham on the other side.

The other tablecloth, shown on the table on the deck (page 95), is made in much the same way but is not reversible. It uses strips of fabric featuring panels of large and small shells sewn on in diagonal lines to form diamond shapes of the backing fabric.

YOU WILL NEED

FOR REVERSIBLE TABLECLOTH
MAIN FABRIC SUCH AS BLUE LINEN
SECOND FABRIC SUCH AS BLUE GINGHAM
MATCHING SEWING THREAD
FLANNEL OR BATTING FOR INTERLINING

FOR SHELL MOTIF TABLECLOTH
MAIN FABRIC SUCH AS SMALL PRINT
SECOND FABRIC SUCH AS LARGE SHELL MOTIF
THIRD FABRIC SUCH AS SMALL SHELL MOTIF

Reversible tablecloth

1 Cut one rectangle from the blue fabric to the desired dimensions. Cut a rectangle of the same size from the interlining. Cut the backing piece of gingham, making it the size of the tablecloth plus 3½in (9cm) all around.

2 Decide how many lengthwise and crosswise strips you will need (allowing for the fact that the gingham around the edge is part of the backing piece, which is brought around to the front to bind the edges). Cut the strips from the gingham, making them 3½in (9cm) wide and as long as the length or width of the tablecloth.

3 Place the interlining on the wrong side of the gingham rectangle, and center the blue linen rectangle over that, right side up. Pin and baste the gingham, interlining, and blue linen together all around the edges and at regular intervals across the center.

4 Press under ¼in (6mm) along both long edges of each gingham strip. Position the crosswise strips, right sides up, on the blue linen side of the tablecloth, remembering to allow for the gingham border all around the edge. Space them equally, making sure they are all straight, and matching the raw ends with the raw edges of the tablecloth. Topstitch along the turned-under edges. Repeat for the lengthwise strips. Remove all basting.

5 Press under ½in (1.25cm) on all four raw edges of the gingham backing. Bring the excess fabric over to the front, folding it along the edge of the linen. Press and topstitch in place. To miter each corner, turn in the corner and trim off the point before folding the straight edges forward. Slipstitch the edges of each corner.

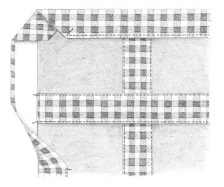

Shell motif tablecloth

1 Cut out one rectangle of the main fabric to the desired dimensions plus ¼in (6mm) all around. Cut wide strips bearing the large shell motif and narrow strips bearing the small shell motif, making them long enough to fit diagonally across the tablecloth. Cut four more narrow strips for the edging, making two of them as long as the length of the fabric rectangle and the other two as long as its width.

2 Find the diagonal of the tablecloth by turning up one corner to the right side so that the end is even with the side. Mark along the diagonal fold with pins. Unfold the fabric. Repeat for the other diagonal.

3 Turn under and press ¼in (6mm) along both long edges of each strip. Position the wide and narrow strips alternately, parallel to one of the pinned diagonal lines and spaced equally. Pin

and baste in place, trimming off the raw ends so they are ¼in (6mm) inside the edge of the tablecloth and parallel to it. Topstitch each strip along both long edges.

4 Press ¼in (6mm) to the *right* side along each edge of the tablecloth. Turn under ¼in (6mm) on all four raw edges of the edging strips. Pin and baste to the edges of the tablecloth, with the wrong side of the strips facing the right side of the tablecloth. Stitch along all four edges of each edging strip. Remove any visible basting.

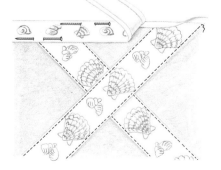

CHAPTER SIX

Bedrooms

With their connotations of luxury, comfort, and relaxation, bedrooms are often the only rooms in the house that can be decorated with more indulgence than practicality. You can choose colors that might not suit the public rooms of the house, such as hot pinks or bright yellows, and really indulge your whims when selecting patterned fabrics and wallpapers. You can fill a bedroom with precious antique textiles or create a romantic fantasy with a four-poster bed or muslin canopy.

When planning the decorative scheme of a bedroom, there are several factors to take into account. As well as the decorating questions that apply to any room in the house, and which are explained in detail in Chapter One, consider how you will be using the room. Will it only be a room to sleep in, will it double as a dressing room, or will it be used for sitting or working in too? Think about the bed, which will probably be the largest object in the room and therefore the main focus of attention. You may decide to invest in a completely new bed or buy a different headboard, or beautiful antique quilt around which you can plan the rest of the decoration. Other antique textiles, such as old carpets, can also form the basis of a room's decorative scheme.

If you want to use bright colors, they should not be so vibrant that the bedroom loses its relaxing atmosphere. Bright blues and greens are more soothing than bright scarlet, strong flame red, or chrome yellow. If you want to use any of the latter colors, opt for slightly muted shades, combine them with plenty of white, or use them only in small amounts, Pale pinks and roses, primrose and cowslip yellows, and sapphire blues are, of course, classic colors for bedrooms.

This colorful bedroom (see pages 100–101) incorporates a classic combination of checks and stripes, illustrating how important it is when combining patterns to use those which work successfully together.

INTRODUCING PATTERN

Very feminine floral prints are classic choices for bedrooms, especially if they are evocative of the past. You can cover the walls with luxuriant climbing roses, extravagant chinoiserie birds and flowers, tendrils of leaves and berries, or romantic bouquets of flowers. There is a wealth of floral prints to choose from, in a variety of finishes that include glazed chintz for a sophisticated look, linen with its tactile, slightly rough texture, and cotton for a simple, rustic atmosphere. Florals are lovely in bedrooms but what started out as a flowery bower can become a claustrophobic swirl of pattern if you get too carried away.

Combine florals with plain fabrics for a classic, traditional look, or opt for the more contemporary combination of florals with stripes or checks. To give the scheme cohesion, choose stripes or checks that pick up the main colors in the florals and try to match two or three of the colors.

Alternatively, you could combine the florals with a fabric that looks plain from a distance yet in fact has a small pattern, such as a tiny sprig or minute check. This not only creates interest, it also prevents the scheme from becoming too busy or fussy, which can be a particular problem in small rooms.

Of course, patterns for bedrooms do not have to be predominantly floral. If you still want a garden-like atmosphere, you could choose a pattern of leaves, berries, or fruits instead of flowers, very small floral motifs with stripes, a subtle overall sprig, or tiny leaves or flowers that form a large trellis pattern, also suggesting the outdoors. It is always worthwhile looking at all the colors a patterned fabric comes in, since a change of palette can make the pattern look completely different.

Checks and stripes are particularly suitable for a more contemporary look, especially if you use large patterns in bold colors. Blues and whites create a crisp, fresh look that is perfect with plain Scandinavian furniture. Choose a simple striped fabric for the curtains, bed linen in a combination of large and small checks, and throws and cushions using the same colors but different checks. For a completely different look, use very little pattern in most of the room but fill some areas with color and texture by choosing boldly patterned throws and rugs for the floor and even the walls.

INTRODUCING TEXTURE

Bedrooms contain so much fabric, in the form of bed linen and curtains, that soft-textured items usually predominate, so it is important to strike a harmonious balance between the soft and hard textures. Even if you want to create a bedroom that is very feminine, you still need a few hard-textured items to provide a contrast with the prevailing softness. Tapestries or antique quilts hung on a wall, and a collection of silver-backed hairbrushes on a fabric-skirted dressing table are classic combinations.

Combine texture with pattern, such as in a colorful rag rug, or allow the texture to form its own pattern, as in a damask fabric. Sheer fabrics, which include muslins, lace, and figured voiles, add marvelously delicate texture when used as window treatments in bedrooms, but they may have to be combined with shades or curtains in a thicker fabric if privacy is an important consideration. Linen is a good choice for curtains in a country-style bedroom, because its heavy texture goes well with stone walls and beams, while glazed cottons and chintzes are ideal for sunny rooms with big windows.

If you want to introduce texture to the bedroom walls, use a paper with a very subtle pattern or a glazed effect. These papers catch the light and create a warm texture. Alternatively, paint the walls and then drag, sponge, or stipple them to introduce texture and, perhaps, a hint of a second color. If the room has rough-plastered or uneven walls and the house has a cottage-like feel, a flat latex, calcimine, or milk paint will enhance the surface texture. The best treatment for tongue-and-groove paneling is often white or cream paint to highlight the play of light and shade across the wooden boards.

Texture can also be introduced through the furniture. Headboards always make a very strong visual statement, whether they are made from ironwork, polished or natural wood, bamboo, or cane or are painted or upholstered. Chests of drawers are usually made from polished wood, which has a soft, lustrous texture that emphasizes

the wood's characteristic grain, but you can create your own effects with paint and paper.

Interesting textures can also be added to a room with accessories. Embroidered bed linen provides pattern, color, and texture. An arrangement of attractively shaped and colored glass bottles can look wonderful on a dressing table, as does a display of colored glass on a windowsill.

In fact, there are a multitude of ways to display bedroom accessories. Arrange wicker baskets, straw hats, wooden painted animals, and other treasured collections on shelves or tables. To dress up their functional nature, decorate hat boxes with wallpaper or fabric, lidded cardboard boxes with paper or paint, and baskets with fabric linings. Paint laundry hampers and upholster their tops.

A detail of the checked bedspread on pages 104–105 shows the lovely, slightly nubbly texture of this colorful linen check fabric, woven in India.

PINK AND YELLOW BEDROOM

Two very different bedroom treatments are shown in this chapter, to illustrate how diverse pattern and texture can be. The first, a sunny bedroom that overlooks a leafy garden, features a classic combination of a striking spaced-floral fabric with a wide bold stripe. The main colors are a deep pink and a clear cowslip yellow, which can be difficult to combine successfully unless both colors have the same intensity. The shades used in this room are gently evocative of the 1950s, giving a contemporary twist to what is really a traditional decorative scheme — as does the painterly style of the floral print. The warmth of the pink and yellow is tempered by the use of white on the ceiling, the white background of the floral print, the candy-striped walls in pink and white, and the white-painted woodwork.

The striped walls were the starting point for the design of the room. This striped effect not only gives definition to the floral curtains by accentuating their pink flowers but provides an optical illusion, making the ceiling appear higher than it really is. Horizontal stripes, on the other hand, would have made the ceiling look lower.

The main focal point of the room is the bedspread, which combines plain areas of color with an outer border and backing of large checks. This pink and yellow checked motif also

Our pink and yellow bedroom is an example of how classic English country style can be interpreted in a contemporary way by combining a bold floral print with equally bold stripes and checks and a strong but fresh color scheme.

appears in a smaller, diagonal pattern in the bed linen, on the window seats, and on the pleated lampshade. The ceiling and woodwork around the windows have been painted white to provide a refreshing contrast to the patterns and colors in the rest of the room.

The yellow in the various fabrics is echoed by the cheerful, painted washstand (which has been used here as a dressing table), chairs, and headboard. Painting inexpensive furniture picked up at a secondhand shop emphasizes its

architectural outlines and insures that it fits in with the rest of the decorative scheme – natural wood would have diminished the intensely colorful character of this room.

The hard edges of the washstand have been softened with a vase of flowers and a pot of trailing ivy which forms a small area of complex pattern against the yellow-painted background. The green and yellow padded fabric picture frames on the washstand serve as decorative accents and also echo the colors of the ivy.

PILLOWCASES WITH BUTTONED OPENINGS

As a contrast to the large checks of the bedspread, the pillowcases in this room are made with a small pink, yellow, and white checked cotton printed on the bias. This gives extra interest to the pillowcases and forms a pleasing contrast with the regular shapes of the larger checks, which are printed on the straight grain, and with the vertical stripes of the walls.

Instead of the usual open end through which the pillow is inserted, these pillowcases have button fastenings at both ends. The buttons are covered with the raspberry-pink fabric which has been used for the bedspread and so the pillowcases echo its color. The wide flanges at either end of the pillowcases provide borders for the buttons and make the pillows look wider than they really are.

When decorating pillowcases with buttons in this way, it is important to place them at the edges of the pillowcase so that you do not actually have to rest your head on the buttons.

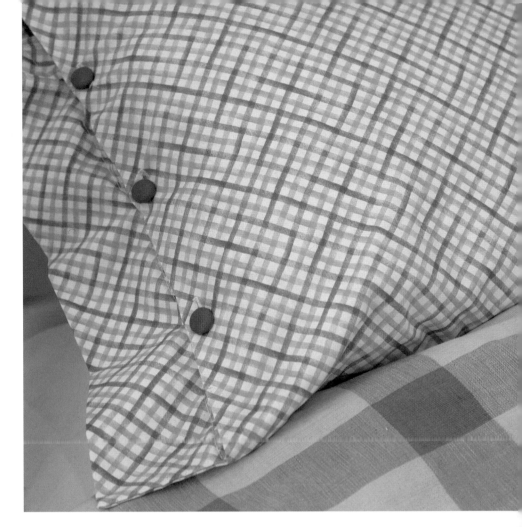

YOU WILL NEED

PILLOW

MAIN FABRIC SUCH AS A SMALL CHECK

SECOND FABRIC IN PLAIN COLOR FOR
COVERING BUTTONS

MATCHING SEWING THREAD

¾IN (2CM) COVERED BUTTON KIT

MEASURING

For the back, cut out a rectangle of fabric 3in (7.5cm) deeper and 25in (63.5cm) wider than your pillow. For the front, cut out a rectangle of fabric 3in (7.5cm) deeper and 8in (20.5cm) wider than the pillow. These dimensions include an allowance of 2in (5cm) each way for ease. Cut the fabric out on the straight grain.

1 Turn under a double 1½in (4cm) hem on each end of the front; hand sew.

2 On the front, make three buttonholes, ½in (1.25cm) from the edge, spacing them so that they are equidistant from the top and bottom edges and from each other.

3 Turn under a double ½in (1.25cm) hem on each end of the back; machine stitch. Mark a line 7in (18cm) from

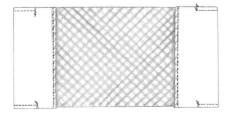

each hemmed end and fold the ends in, right sides together, along these lines. Stitch a ½in (1.25cm) seam halfway across the top and bottom on each side as shown. Clip into each seam allowance at the point where the stitching stops. Trim off the corners, turn right side out, and press.

4 Topstitch each side between the clips in the seam allowances, stitching through both layers.

5 Place the front and back with right sides together, aligning the sides of the front with the topstitching on the back. Stitch a ½in (1.25cm) seam along the top and bottom edges, stitching through the flaps on the back at the same time. Turn the pillowcase right side out and press.

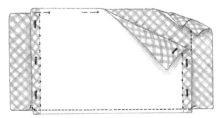

6 Cover the buttons following the manufacturer's directions. Sew them to the back, sewing only through the inner flap on each side.

CHECKED BEDSPREAD

This bedspread, which incorporates the main design themes of the room, successfully combines areas of pattern and solid color, with the solid colors arranged to form a pattern of their own. The central yellow panel highlights the yellow painted furniture, while the thick pink stripe echoes the stripes on the walls and also defines the shape of the bed. The bold border of large pink and yellow tonal checks combines well with the equally bold stripes. This fabric is also used for the slipper chair and one of the cushions on the window seat. As a general rule, try to bring in each pattern at least twice when mixing patterns, otherwise the room will lack a cohesive design.

The checked fabric forms the underside of the bedspread, making it reversible. The two layers are held in place with large yellow buttons sewn onto each corner of the yellow and pink panels. You could use buttons in any of the colors that feature in the bedspread.

The checked fabric is a heavy woven cotton from India, and the two plain fabrics are also heavy woven cottons.

MEASURING

To decide the finished width of the bedspread, measure the top of your bed and the height from the floor (or from wherever you want the bedspread to stop). The finished width should be the width of the bed plus *twice* the height; the finished length should be the length of the bed plus the height plus about 6in (15cm) to allow for pillows.

For the underside of the bedspread, cut out a rectangle from the checked fabric (joining widths if necessary) to the finished dimensions plus ½in (1.25cm) seam allowances all around.

For the top, use the finished dimensions to work out the size of each section. You'll need a central panel, four pink strips to surround the yellow panel, and four checked strips to surround them. In each case add a ½in (1.25cm) seam allowance to the edge. When you cut out the checked strips, be sure to match the pattern.

1 With right sides together, stitch a pink strip to each edge of the yellow rectangle, taking a ½in (1.25cm) seam, and starting and stopping at the seamlines of the adjacent edges. Press the pink strips away from the yellow rectangle. Miter each corner by stitching with right sides together from the end of the stitching to the outside edge on the diagonal. Press.

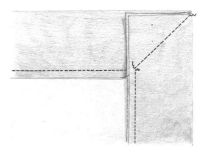

2 Join the checked strips to the pink strips in the same way, mitering the corners carefully so that the pattern matches around the corner.

3 Place the front and back with right sides together and raw edges even. Stitch a ½in (1.25cm) seam all around, leaving an opening in the top edge, where it will be the least conspicuous. Turn the bedspread right side out through the opening, press and then slipstitch the opening to close.

4 Sew buttons onto the corners between the yellow and pink fabrics, and between the pink and checked fabrics, sewing through all layers.

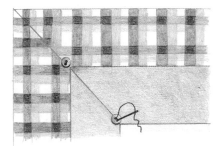

EMBROIDERED FABRIC FRAMES

Padded frames like these are simple to make and a marvelous way of adding personalized accessories to a room and accenting your color scheme. They also make lovely presents for family and friends, especially if you choose colors that will suit the recipient's house and include a photograph they particularly like. Textured linen weaves in lime and cowslip yellow were chosen for the frames, and the hand embroidery provides extra texture and pattern.

You could use various sewing threads, such as glossy embroidery floss or matte embroidery cotton, crewel yarn, or button thread, according to the fabric you have chosen and the style of the room for which the frames are intended. Experiment with different embroidery stitches, or make up your own. Combining raised stitches with flat ones works well, as does using one stitch to make a border for another. If you are using a stitch for the first time, test it out on a scrap piece of fabric until you are absolutely sure of what you are doing.

YOU WILL NEED

HEAVY CARDBOARD SUCH AS MAT BOARD OR MOUNTING BOARD
CARPENTER'S SQUARE (OR SQUARE CORNER SUCH AS A CD CASE OR A BOOK)
METAL RULER
X-ACTO KNIFE OR MAT KNIFE
HEAVYWEIGHT BATTING
FABRIC SUCH AS LINEN
CONTRASTING EMBROIDERY FLOSS
WHITE CRAFT GLUE OR FABRIC GLUE
CELLOPHANE TAPE
SMALL PIECE OF FUSIBLE WEB

1 Using a carpenter's square, metal ruler, and X-acto knife or mat knife, cut out two pieces of heavy cardboard to the desired frame size. Cut out a window in one piece, for the front.

2 Cut out a piece of heavyweight batting just like the cardboard front, and glue it to the cardboard.

3 On the wrong side of the fabric, draw around both cardboard pieces, then cut 1in (2.5cm) outside the marked lines. Cut off the points from the outer corners and cut diagonally into the inner corners, almost to the marked lines.

4 Embroider the fabric using 1, 2, or 3 strands of contrasting embroidery floss, depending on the effect you prefer. We have used running stitch, cross stitch, and French knots, all shown in the following illustration.

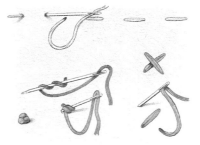

5 Center the cardboard front on the wrong side of the fabric, batting side down. Fold the inner and outer fabric seam allowances to the back of the cardboard. Glue at the back, and also secure with cellophane tape.

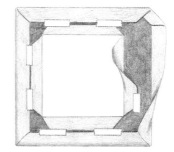

6 Center the cardboard back on the wrong side of the larger fabric rectangle. Fold the fabric seam allowances to the back of the card-board. Glue in place. Cover with the remaining rectangle, fixing it in place with glue.

7 Glue the front to the back around the edges only, leaving the top edge of the frame free of glue.

8 For the stand, cut a small piece of cardboard and cover it with fabric as in step 6. Attach with a fabric loop made from two small fabric strips joined with fusible web; glue the ends together then fold and glue to the back of the frame and to the stand. Slide the picture in through the top of the frame.

WINDOW SEAT CUSHIONS

YOU WILL NEED

FOAM OR BOX CUSHION FORM
FABRIC FOR CUSHION
PLAIN FABRIC FOR ROSETTES AND
FOR COVERED BUTTONS
MATCHING SEWING THREAD
PIPING CORD
COVERED BUTTONS
PINKING SHEARS
UPHOLSTERY THREAD
LONG UPHOLSTERY NEEDLE

The two window seats are among the most attractive features of this bedroom and this treatment makes the most of them. The pink, yellow, and white checked fabric from which the pillowcases are made has been used for these window seat cushions, and its bias-printed design is especially dramatic against the white-painted wood paneling in this confined space. For extra definition the edges have been piped with the same checked fabric cut on the bias. To match the button motifs on the bed linen, buttons covered with the raspberry-pink fabric of the bedspread, with rosettes made from the same fabric, have been sewn onto both sides of the cushions.

MEASURING

Cut two rectangles of fabric to the width and length of your foam or cushion form plus ½in (1.25cm) all around for seam allowances.

For the gusset, cut two strips as wide as the cushion height plus 1in (2.5cm) and as long as the cushion width plus 1in (2.5cm). Cut two more to the same width, and as long as the cushion length plus 1in (2.5cm) for seam allowances.

1 Make bias binding from the main fabric and use it to prepare the piping (see page 44, steps 6, 7, and 8), making enough to pipe all around the top and bottom of the cushion.

2 With raw edges even, and the zipper foot on the machine, stitch the piping to the right side of each rectangle. At the corners, clip into the seam allowance of the piping. Join the ends at the back of each piece by trimming the ends of the cord to just meet, then

turning under one end of the bias binding and wrapping it over the other.

3 Join the ends of the gusset strips with ½in (1.25cm) seams, starting and stopping ½in (1.25cm) from each end. Check that this ring fits around the cushion or foam exactly.

4 With right sides together and raw edges even, pin the gusset all around one of the piped rectangles, matching corners. With the zipper foot on the machine, stitch a ½in (1.25cm) seam all around. Trim the seams and trim off the corners on the rectangle. Repeat for the other piped rectangle, leaving the back edge open this time. Turn right side out and press.

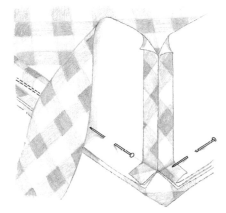

5 Insert the foam or cushion form through the opening in the seam, and slipstitch the opening to close.

6 To make a rosette for each button, fold a small square of fabric into quarters, and then cut out a quarter-circle through all four layers using pinking shears.

7 Measure and mark out the position of the covered buttons and rosettes on the cushion with pins.

8 Thread a long upholstery needle with upholstery thread. At the first button position, push the needle through the cushion from the bottom to the top, holding onto the loose end of the thread. Thread it through a rosette circle, then through the button shank, and then back through the rosette. Take it back down to the bottom and thread it through another rosette circle and button in the same way. Tie the ends in a slip knot at the bottom. Fasten off the ends. Repeat for each button and rosette.

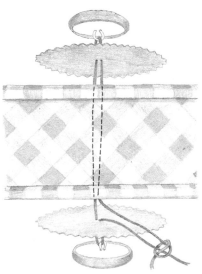

STRIPED WALLS

The walls in this room are deceptive at first glance because they appear to be covered in wallpaper. It is only when you take a closer look that you realize the effect is achieved solely with paint. To re-create this look, first apply two coats of the white background, then, when the second coat is thoroughly dry, paint on the pink stripes, using masking tape to achieve the straight lines.

To create the attractive texture of these stripes, use a slightly diluted latex paint. Then, after it has dried, paint an acrylic glaze over the stripes. Before the glaze has dried, drag a long, soft-bristled brush through the glaze from top to bottom. You will have to work quickly, because water-based glazes dry very rapidly.

You need a fairly even wall surface if you are going to create this striped effect with paint. Most walls have a few gentle curves, especially in old houses, but any serious irregularities might make it difficult to keep the stripes straight.

It's worth experimenting with different stripes beforehand. The width of these stripes was based on a Laura Ashley wallpaper. You could use a wallpaper for reference or design your own pattern, choosing stripes of a size that complements the room. Making the colored stripes narrower or wider than the white ones produces very different effects.

Of course, you do not have to give the stripes a white background – you might want to use cobalt blue stripes on a sapphire background, butter yellow ones on a primrose background, or mint on a jade background for a more subtle, "tonal" painted stripe. You can also combine completely different colors, as long as they have the same intensity of color – rich yellow and smoky blue would look good – although a combination of brighter colors, such as emerald and scarlet, might be very hard to live with.

Whatever you choose, practice painting the stripes first on a sheet of lining paper or plain wallpaper, then tape this to the wall so you can see how the design looks and make any necessary adjustments. Drape the curtain fabric beside the paper and scrutinize the effect both in daylight and artificial light.

Before you begin to paint, study the room for architectural focal points, just as if you were hanging wallpaper, because these will be the starting point when positioning the stripes. A fireplace may be the focal point or the main feature may be an expanse of wall framed by two floor-to-ceiling windows, as in this room. Center the stripes over the focal point, using a plumb line to make sure your measurements are accurate and your stripes straight, and then work outward in each direction. This may mean the stripes are not quite equal at either end of the room – unfortunately, not every architectural focal point is always exactly centered – but it will not be obvious because your eye will automatically be drawn to the central feature.

When the stripes eventually meet, they will probably not form a perfect match. To prevent this mismatch from being too obvious, try to make the unequal stripes meet in the darkest or most hidden part of the room, such as behind a door or in a shadowy recess.

ORCHARD BEDROOM

This fresh, airy bedroom belongs to a house set on the bank of a river. The owners wanted their room to be an extension of the leafy view seen through the French doors leading onto the balcony – in other words, to bring the outdoors indoors. The corner housing the bed has been decorated to resemble an orchard, with stylized apple trees painted directly on the off-white walls. The curtains, with their wisteria pattern, echo this rural atmosphere and are arranged to puddle in delicate folds on the floor.

The furniture also evokes an outdoor theme and provides the main textural focus of the room, with a headboard that looks like an orchard gate and chairs that would not be out of place in a garden. A simple, white-painted bench provides additional seating under the smaller of the two windows, and its striped cushions complement the green slats of the garden chairs. The table beside the bench is an old metal one, also intended for garden use, whose look has been softened with a pretty, embroidered tablecloth. The original verdigris of its legs blends perfectly with the other greens in the room. A length of white-painted garden trellis has been used to camouflage the radiator.

Simple cottage flowers continue the garden theme, with daisies in a bucket in the fireplace, and other small pots of flowers displayed in old wooden seed trays and garden baskets.

This bedroom was inspired by a country orchard with a lovely white painted gate, baskets of apples, and fresh meadow flowers growing among the trees.

ORCHARD GATE HEADBOARD

If you can't find a suitable headboard for your bedroom, don't give up hope – you can always make your own from the most unexpected sources. This headboard started out as a piece of garden trellis, its curved top already in place. All that needed to be added were the two newel posts, originally intended for banisters, and their decorative finials, all of which were nailed in place. L-shaped brackets secured the posts to the trellis, and the headboard to the bed. If you decide to copy this idea, make sure that you buy a sturdy piece of trellis – anything flimsy will not stand up well to continual use.

When the headboard has been assembled, the wood has to be rubbed down with sandpaper because it will be rather rough. This may seem a painstaking and lengthy job but it is worth doing well because the end results are so pleasing. When the wood is ready, prepare it for painting by applying a wood primer and leaving it to dry. Finally, apply an undercoat followed by a top coat of paint.

A piece of garden trellis can also be used to make a simple bulletin board by nailing it onto a piece of hardboard and painting it a suitable color. Letters, postcards, appointment cards, bills, and other reminders can then be tucked between the pieces of trellis.

STENCILED TREES

The stencils used in this room are unusual in that they are combined with hand painting to show large, representational objects rather than small areas of repeated motifs.

Buy ready-made stencils from specialist shops or make your own from stencil card. Stencils can be applied with various types of paint including car spray paint. Using this involves masking off a large area around the stencil itself, so you may prefer to use stencil paints instead. These have a relatively dry consistency to stop them dripping or running under the stencil, and are sold in a good range of colors. Stencil crayons are also available, or just use standard latex paint, applying it with a brush or sponge.

Part of the charm of stencils lies in their rough finish, so aim to apply the paint in a patchy

texture. If it goes on too evenly, wait for it to dry and then lightly rub it down with sandpaper.

When stencils are used in areas that receive a lot of wear, such as hallways, landings, and living rooms, they need to be protected with a layer of flat varnish that will not yellow with age. Such protection is not normally needed in a bedroom.

1 Draw a variety of apple and leaf shapes on stencil card. Place the card on a cutting mat or thick cardboard and cut out the stencils using a sharp X-acto knife or mat knife. Hold the knife upright and always cut toward you holding the card steady with your other hand behind the blade. To cut curves, turn the card not the knife.

2 Working on a white-painted wall, lightly trace the outlines of the tree trunks first. Paint the trunks quite roughly, using the flat brush for the wider areas and the medium and fine brushes for the narrow parts and tips of the branches.

3 When the paint is dry, back the surface with fine sandpaper or a sanding block so that the white paint shows through in places.

4 Using only a very small amount of paint in the different greens, stencil apples and leaves among the branches. Tape the stencil in position and hold it with your free hand while you stencil with the other hand. Hold the brush at right angles to the wall and use it in a light, circular action. Start at the edges, applying the paint more densely there and fading it away at the center, to create a three-dimensional effect of shadows and highlights. On some of the apples, add variety by using a lighter color for the highlighting, or a deeper color for the shadows.

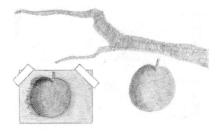

LACE PILLOWS

A bed piled high with a mound of pillows creates a welcoming sense of luxury and relaxation, especially if the cushions are covered with attractive fabrics and antique textiles. Lace cushions are among the most luxurious choices of all, whether the lace you use is brand new, is a treasured family heirloom, or has been bought from an antique shop or market.

Instead of lace panels, use old lace tray cloths, as shown on pages 49–50, either folded in half or used as they are and with cushion pads bought to fit them. You can also make much smaller cushions from lace handkerchiefs, or one large cushion from several lace handkerchiefs stitched together to form a delicate patchwork.

If you are a skilled embroiderer, buy lace cushion covers with linen panels on which to stitch your own designs. Or decorate plain pieces of fabric by stitching strips of lace on them in interesting patterns.

GARDEN BENCH WITH CUSHIONS

This was originally a small, two-seater garden bench, but the addition of simple cushions has turned it into suitable seating for a bedroom. Like the trellis-turned-headboard, the wood was sanded down before being given a couple of coats of white paint. Long ties at the corners of the seat cushion and three ties spaced along the top of the backrest insure that the cushions are held firmly in place. You can also adapt this idea for the seating in a conservatory or garden room, perhaps making cushions for wooden chairs as well as a garden bench.

The fabric chosen for this room is a bold green-and-white ticking, which resembles the type of fabric traditionally used for deckchairs. The fabric helps to give definition to the green of the curtains.

For a similar effect, use large checks or a simple gingham instead of this green and white stripe. A floral fabric will give a very different look – a floral print similar to the one used for the curtains would look very traditional and pretty, while a brightly colored floral fabric in a contemporary pattern would be striking and dramatic, especially if you painted the bench in an equally vivid color, like scarlet. Such color schemes are unsuitable for this room, of course, but would look marvelous in a large and busy hallway or a sunny garden room.

If you intend to remove the cushions for washing, insert zippers at the base of the top cushion and at the back of the seat, so that they are hidden from view. For a larger bench, you could make box cushions (see pages 108–109), which would be thicker and therefore provide more padding.

YOU WILL NEED

FABRIC SUCH AS TICKING
MATCHING SEWING THREAD
PIPING CORD
THIN FOAM OR HEAVYWEIGHT BATTING

MEASURING

Measure the length and depth of the seat; and cut foam or batting to these dimensions. For the size of the fabric pieces, add the thickness of the foam or batting plus 1in (2.5cm) for seam allowances to each dimension. Do the same for the back.

1 Cut out two pieces of fabric for each, making a paper pattern (see page 44, step 1) of the front corners of the seat, and using this to shape the front of the cushion around the struts.

2 Cut out bias strips from the fabric and make into piping (see page 44, steps 6, 7, and 8). With raw edges even, stitch the piping around the edge of one back piece and one seat piece on the right side. For the seat, start and stop on each side of the front corners; at the other corners, clip into the seam allowance of the piping so it will fit easily around the corner.

3 For the ties, cut out on the straight grain 18 strips of fabric, each 2 x 15in (5 x 38cm). Turn under ¼in (6mm) on both long edges and one end, then fold in half lengthwise, with wrong sides together. Stitch down the side and across the turned-under end.

4 With raw edges even, baste the ties in pairs to the right side of each piped piece at the corners, just inside the seamline. Also baste a pair of ties in the middle of the top edge of the back.

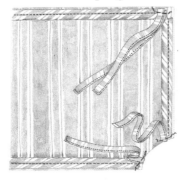

5 Baste the other seat piece to the piped piece, right sides together. With the zipper foot on the machine, stitch a ½in (1.25cm) seam all around the edges, leaving a large opening in the back edge. Trim seam, clip corners, and remove basting.

6 Turn the seat cover right side out and press. Insert the foam or basting through the opening, and slipstitch the opening closed. Repeat the procedure for the back cushion, positioning the opening in the lower edge.

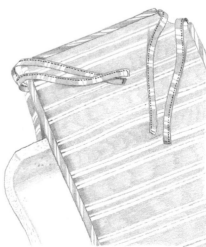

PLANTS IN POTS

The leafy green quality of this bedroom is enhanced by the flowering plants that decorate the windowsill, fireplace, and bedside tables. If you have interesting containers like an old enamel bucket or wooden garden basket, fill them with suitable flowering plants that will flourish indoors. These include white marguerites, geraniums, cosmos, marigolds, pansies, and bulbs such as small irises and hyacinths. When they have finished flowering, simply replace them with something new.

DISTRESSED DOOR

Distressing paintwork to make it look time-worn is one of the easiest techniques of decorating with paint. It imitates an antique finish, creating in a relatively short time what would normally take years of wear and tear to achieve. It can also be used to "age" a piece of furniture or other wooden item, such as a door or fireplace, that is not really old at all. For this door, a top coat of forest green has been lightly sanded in places to reveal an ocher undercoat.

1 To distress paintwork, first strip off all the old paint or varnish until you have reached the wood. If you are planning to distress a piece of polished wood, remove all traces of the polish with fine steel wool and then wash down the surface with mineral spirits.

2 Apply the undercoat and leave it to dry, followed by the top coat in whichever color you have chosen.

3 When the topcoat has dried, start to rub away areas of paint, using fine steel wool, to create a suitably aged finish. This looks most convincing when you concentrate on the areas

that would naturally receive the most wear, such as around handles, corners, and edges. Every now and then, stand back from your work to see how it is progressing and to gain an overview of the general effect.

4 When you are pleased with the result, protect your work with a layer of polyurethane varnish or, for a more natural-looking finish, apply a thin layer of furniture polish or wax, leaving it for about 30 minutes before buffing it to a shine with a duster.

CHAPTER SEVEN

Outdoor Living

One of the great pleasures of summer is being able to spend most of the day outside, whether you are reading, relaxing, working, or gardening. It is especially enjoyable and relaxing being able to eat al fresco and to entertain friends and family on your balcony or deck or in the garden. Although part of the charm of outdoor eating is its simplicity, it should not be so basic that it becomes difficult to manage the meal neatly and elegantly. You may be eating outdoors but you still need to provide sturdy tables, comfortable chairs, suitable shading from the sun, and that most elusive item of all – a sense of occasion.

If you want your summer living to be memorable, forget all about plastic plates, paper napkins, plastic chairs, and other so-called labor-saving inventions. Instead, you can spend the long winter evenings anticipating the joys of the summer to come by stitching your own napkins and tablecloths, re-covering deckchairs and director's chairs if need be, making seat covers for upright outdoor chairs and collecting some suitably summery crockery – large pottery bowls to hold salads and pasta, boldly colored dinner plates, and big platters for cheeses. For evening entertaining al fresco, combine them with colorful glass containers for night lights, or lanterns hung from trees.

A garden terrace abundant with foliage and bursting with flowers in the height of summer provides a wonderful dining "room" for entertaining en plein air.

CHOOSING A THEME

If you wish, you can choose a theme for your summer table – Mediterranean, aglow with bright colors and vivid patterns; Edwardian English, with an elegant tablecloth, embroidered napkins, and pretty floral china, which is especially suitable for tea parties; or colonial, with wicker chairs and tables, old blue and white plates, and a checked tablecloth. Your table will be the centerpiece of your decorative scheme, especially if you will be using a mixture of different pieces of furniture.

If you are really enthusiastic about a particular theme, you could even plant shrubs and flowers that reflect it. Lots of old-fashioned roses, honeysuckle, and cottage-garden flowers would suit an English theme; lilies, poppies, sunflowers, and delphiniums could be used with a colonial theme; and sun-loving plants such as cistus, lavender, rosemary, and nasturtiums would create a Mediterranean atmosphere.

Even just a few strategically placed pots and tubs of flowers will help to set the scene, especially if you choose scented varieties. You might even want to grow a few pots of herbs near the eating area, so guests can pick small sprigs of borage or mint to put in their drinks, or sprinkle freshly picked oregano or basil on their food. Such ideas are very simple but they will greatly increase the sense of atmosphere, and therefore your enjoyment.

MIXING COLORS AND PATTERNS

You can use colors for outdoor living that you might never consider for indoors, where they could be too bright. Scarlets, oranges, limes, bright yellows, hot pinks, jade greens, and cobalt blues all look good in an outdoor setting because they stand up well to the strong sunlight of a hot summer's day. Each chair could be covered in a fabric of a different color, or, for a more cohesive look, a set of chairs could be decorated so that two chairs feature each color. You can use the same idea when choosing crockery.

Fabrics in bold patterns also work well outdoors, especially bright checks, bold stripes, and vivid florals. Alternatively, there are many subtle designs available if you want to create a more restrained look. In fact, you might prefer to keep the colors and patterns very simple and choose furniture that provides most of the texture and interest. And you may want to choose fabrics that blend well with your garden – here the classic English florals, and the yellows, pinks, greens, and blues sit beautifully in this traditional English flower garden. Some cane and wicker chairs, both new and antique, need no more adornment than a simple cushion.

For informal al fresco meals, choose a spot in the shade of a tree. At dusk hang lanterns from the branches of the tree to create a romantic setting for enjoying mellow summer evenings.

SUMMER GARDEN

There are three different eating areas in this decorative scheme – one, with a pretty tent (see left), is ideal for a smart cocktail party; another is designed for an outdoor dinner or lunch party on the terrace (see pages 120–121 and 130); and a third is perfect for an informal al fresco meal in the shade of a tree (see page 123). All can be adapted to your own requirements, and you can combine elements from each to create the eating area perfect for your garden and your style of entertaining.

The thread that links these three outdoor schemes is their principal colors of cowslip yellow and white, with splashes of green, blue, and pink. The patterns were chosen because they are classic, simple, fresh prints of flowers from an English country garden.

The tent in the drinks area has been covered with cotton chintz in a classic pattern of splashy cowslip yellow roses on a white ground. This smart fabric goes well with the classic shape of the tent and makes it suitable for entertaining. The table is decked with a heavy cotton printed with a yellow and white trefoil pattern, and a nearby deckchair has a cover of yellow and white ticking. In the dining area, six matching garden chairs have been given full-length slipcovers in a pretty cotton chintz in yellow, deep pink, green, and chambray blue. The third area features a combination of checks, plains, and a smaller sprig print in blues, greens, and pinks.

This magical floral tent not only provides a focus for a garden party but also creates a shady spot in which to read and enjoy the pleasures of a summer garden.

FLORAL TENT

This elegant yellow and white floral tent (also shown on previous page) provides not only shade in which to set out your food and drink but also a wonderful focal point for a garden party – as well as a sense of occasion.

The fabric used for both the exterior and the lining is a classic pattern of full-blown roses, but you could choose one pattern for the exterior and something different for the lining.

The framework is a simple construction of battens joined together with wing nuts. Use eight 2in x 1in (5 x 2.5cm) battens to make the four criss-cross pieces (one for each side and two for the back), drilling the holes for the wing nuts. Hammer a 4in (10cm) nail halfway into each end of four sturdy dowels; these will go into the finials at the top and into the ground. Screw the battens to the dowels so one dowel is at each corner (cutting a flat area in the dowel at each screw point). The two dowels and two battens at the front need to be longer because the roof slopes. Strengthen the structure with horizontal

battens running from side to side at the top (front and back). After putting the canopy over the framework, top the four poles with decorative finials. For the guy ropes, cut grooves in four stakes, and drill two holes in four more pieces of wood; use these to fix guy ropes to the tent as shown in the photograph on page 124. To store, unscrew the criss-cross sections from the horizontal battens and dowels, and loosen the wing nuts so the sides and back fold up.

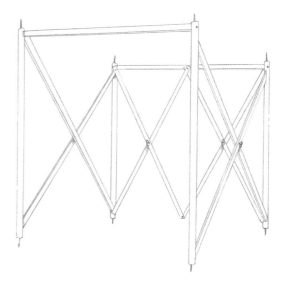

MEASURING

Our tent is 47in (120cm) deep, 90in (229cm) wide, 87in (221cm) high at the front and about 12in (30cm) lower at the back, but yours could easily be bigger or smaller than that. Cut out and, if necessary, join fabric widths to make one wall piece (extending around all three sides) and one roof piece for the outside, and the same for the lining. Allow 1in (2.5cm) for each seam. On the wall piece of both the main fabric and the lining, mark where the corners will be, and cut the top edge of each side part of the wall at an angle so that it will be 12in (30cm) higher at the front than at the back. Cut the back to the lower height. You will also need two valance pieces, one in the main fabric and one in the lining; ours is 15in (38cm) deep. If your fabric has a large pattern, be sure to match it all the way around.

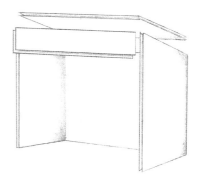

YOU WILL NEED

WOODEN FRAMEWORK WITH GUY ROPES
FABRIC
MATCHING SEWING THREAD
STIFF INTERFACING

1 With right sides together, join the outside wall piece to the lining wall piece along the vertical front edges and the lower edges, taking 1in (2.5cm) seams. Trim off the corners, press the seams open, and turn right side out. Baste around the top edge.

2 With right sides together, baste then stitch the outside roof piece to the top edge of the walls; take a 1in (2.5cm) seam and clip into the seam allowance of the walls at the corners.

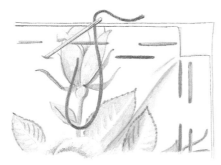

3 If your stiff interfacing is fusible, iron it to the wrong side of one valance piece following the manufacturer's directions. Otherwise, baste it around the seamline on the wrong side. Make a template for the scallops, if possible taking into account the position of the pattern on each scallop – our scallops are each 15in (38cm) wide and follow the pattern repeat. Draw around the template onto the wrong side of the uninterfaced valance piece.

4 Place the two valance pieces with right sides together and stitch along the scallops and up both sides, taking a ¼in (6mm) seam. Trim the seam and clip into the seam allowance on the curves. Turn right side out and press.

5 Join the straight edge of the valance to the front edge of the lining roof, with the underside of the valance facing the right side of the lining.

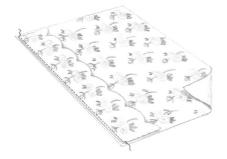

6 Turn under the 1in (2.5cm) seam allowance on the other three edges of the lining roof. With wrong sides together, hand sew it to the underside of the roof piece.

7 Mark the positions of the poles and finials at each corner, and cut holes in the roof for these. Finish the edges with buttonhole stitch, sewing through both layers at once.

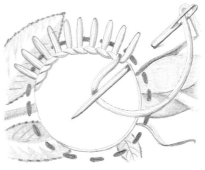

8 Hand sew the ends of the valance to the sides. Remove all basting and press.

YOU WILL NEED

TERRA-COTTA POTS

LATEX PAINT IN WHITE

ACRYLIC PAINTS IN NATURAL, EARTHY
SHADES LIKE BURNT SIENNA, YELLOW
OCHER, RAW SIENNA, BURNT UMBER, AND
CADMIUM RED

SELECTION OF FLAT DECORATOR'S BRUSHES,
1IN (2.5CM) AND 2IN (5CM) WIDE

SPONGES AND RAGS

REPOSITIONABLE SPRAY ADHESIVE

STENCIL CARD AND BRUSH

1 Make sure the pots are clean and free of dust and dirt. Mix 1 part latex with 10 parts water, and paint this over the outside of the pots. It will dry very quickly and look blotchy initially, but this effect will fade as you apply subsequent colors, leaving a soft, misty effect.

2 Dilute the acrylics with water in the same 1:10 ratio (unless you want a deeper, richer color, in which case use less water). Apply the colors with the brushes, using a different brush for each. Experiment with different mixtures of shades, and try one shade on top of another, allowing the paint to dry between coats.

PAINTED TERRA-COTTA POTS

A good way to add character to brand-new terra-cotta pots is to paint them. The pots shown here have been given a variety of treatments, including simple painting and reverse stencils. The colors chosen are all similar to the original terra-cotta, but if you wish you can paint them in bright colors. Give them bold stripes, zigzag patterns, or splotches of color, or paint flowers, stars, or leaves on them. Paint the rim in one color and the body in another, or emphasize raised bands in the terra-cotta with different colors. Don't worry if the colors seem too bright – the weather will soon fade them slightly.

Because the pots can be moved around, they are an excellent way to decorate the part of your garden you want as the focus of a party. They also look very attractive indoors and in conservatories.

3 On some, use the sponge or a rag to distress the painted surface while it is still wet, so that the next color you apply will accentuate the patchiness, to look naturally aged.

4 For the stripes, turn the pot over and allow dribbles of color to run down the sides. When these are dry, apply other shades over the top to make the stripes fainter.

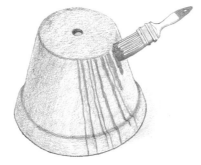

5 For the leaf-patterned pot, cut leafy sprigs from stencil card. Because this is reverse stenciling, you use the cut-out shapes, not the card from which they have been cut. Working in a well-ventilated area, spray the cut-out shapes with the adhesive and stick them in position around the pot. Use a stencil brush to apply the paint around them, then remove the card.

6 To remove any spills on the inside, rub back with sandpaper when the pots are dry. Do not varnish, or you will lose the dry, powdery finish.

PLEATED TABLECLOTH

Light, refreshing breezes are welcome on hot summer days but they can set tablecloths flapping in an annoying way. If you will be sitting around the table you may prefer to dispense with a tablecloth altogether and use placemats instead, but a buffet or drinks table can be given a fitted tablecloth that will sit snugly in place and look extremely decorative.

One of the benefits of this fitted tablecloth is that it hides a multitude of sins. It enables you to use a table that is past its prime, or even a wallpapering table. It also allows you to press into service objects that aren't really tables at all, such as a large desk or even a large piece of wood laid on a smaller table. And you can store empty wine crates, boxes of glasses, emergency plates, and other items out of sight under the table.

MEASURING

For the top, measure the length and width of your tabletop, and add about ⅜in (1cm) to each measurement for ease. Add a further 1in (2.5cm) to both the length and width for seam allowances. Cut out one piece of main fabric to these dimensions. (If your table is very long and you are using a fabric that has to run from top to bottom of each panel, you may need to join widths.)

For the side panels, measure the height of the table and cut two pieces of main fabric as deep as this measurement plus 3in (7.5cm) and as wide as the length of the top fabric piece. Again, you may have to join widths if your table is long.

For the end panels, cut two pieces of main fabric as deep as the side panels, and as wide as the width of the top fabric piece.

For the pleat linings, cut four pieces of striped fabric, 12in (30.5cm) wide and as deep as the panels.

1 Join the widths if necessary to make the top and the side panels.

2 Make up bias binding from the coordinating fabric and prepare enough piping to pipe around the top (see page 44, steps 6, 7, and 8). With right sides together and raw edges even, stitch the piping along all four edges of the top, clipping into the seam allowances of the piping at the corners.

3 For the ties, cut eight 3 x 27in (7.5 x 68.5cm) strips of the main fabric. Turn under ¼in (6mm) along the long edges, fold in half lengthwise, wrong sides together, and press. Cut one end diagonally, turn under ¼in (6mm) on both edges, and press. Stitch down the side and across the pointed end.

4 With right sides together and raw edges even, baste a tie on each edge of the side and end panels, about 11in (28cm) from the top. Position each tie so that the stitched edge runs along the bottom of the tie.

5 With right sides together and raw edges even, pin the side edges of the pleat linings to the side edges of the side and end panels, so that you have one large ring. Stitch, taking ½in (1.25cm) seams. Press the seams open.

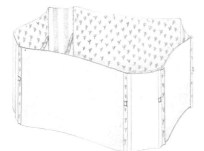

6 At the top, pin the seamlines on either side of the pleat linings with right sides together, turning the seam allowances to opposite sides. Stitch along the seamline for the top 5in (12.5cm), reinforcing the bottom end of the stitching with backstitching. Repeat for the other pleat linings.

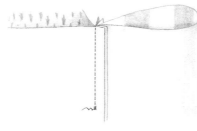

7 Form the pleat linings into inverted pleats. Baste across the top and press.

8 With right sides together and raw edges even, baste the top piece to the pleated ring, matching the corners.

With the zipper foot on the machine, stitch all around, taking a ½in (1.25cm) seam. Trim the seam and corners.

9 Turn up ¼in (6mm) and then 2¼in (6cm) along the lower edge, and hand sew or machine stitch. Turn the tablecloth right side out, remove all basting, and press. Slip over the table and tie each of the pleats together.

COVERS FOR GARDEN CHAIRS

Folding, slatted wood garden chairs are attractive but not very comfortable. Perhaps the simplest cushions to make are these small, thin pads that can be tied on the chair back and seat. The covers are made in a pretty floral print and have a fun, lighthearted look well suited to a bright summer's day. The top cover is folded over the chair back and tied on each side, while the seat cushion is a simple knife-edge cushion, fastened at the back with self-ties.

YOU WILL NEED

FABRIC
MATCHING SEWING THREAD
PIPING CORD
LIGHT OR MEDIUM WEIGHT BATTING

1 Make a paper pattern for the seat cover (see page 44, step 1). Use this pattern to cut out two fabric pieces and one piece of batting for each chair seat, adding ½in (1.25cm) all around for the seam allowances.

2 Make a paper pattern for the back cover by drawing a rectangle large enough to cover the back and extend a little beyond it. Draw three scallops on one edge. Fold the fabric in half, right sides together, and place the straight edge of the pattern on the fold. Draw around the scalloped pattern, adding a ½in (1.25cm) seam allowance to each cut edge. Cut out through both layers.

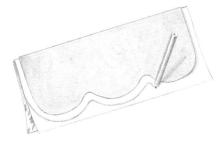

3 Repeat to make a second piece. Cut out a piece of batting in the same way.

4 Make up bias binding and prepare piping (see page 44, steps 6, 7, and 8). With right sides together, stitch the piping around the edges of the seat cover and the back cover. Clip into the seam allowance of the piping on curves and at the corners and join the ends (see page 108, step 2).

5 For the ties, cut out twelve 1¾in x 15in (4.5 x 38cm) strips of fabric on the straight grain. Turn under ¼in (6mm) on each long edge and on one end, and then fold each strip in half lengthwise, wrong sides together. Stitch along the long edge and the folded end. With right sides together and raw edges even, baste a pair of ties near each back corner of one seat cover piece and a single tie at each corner of one back cover piece.

6 Place the other back cover piece over the first, right sides together. Lay the piece of batting on top of that, and baste all around. With the zipper foot on the machine, stitch all around, taking a ½in (1.25cm) seam and leaving an opening in one side. Trim the seam and clip into the seam allowances on the curves. Turn right side out and slipstitch the opening. Remove the basting and press.

7 Repeat step 6 for the seat cover, leaving the opening in the back edge.

8 Fold the back cover in half lengthwise and tie to the chair back. Tie the seat cover onto the seat at the back.

FULL-LENGTH SLIPCOVERS

If you own only one set of garden chairs you can create different covers to change their appearance. These full-length slipcovers have a formal and elegant look that is particularly appropriate for the dining area of the garden, yet in fact they hide the same folding chairs featured in the informal seating area under the tree.

The fabric used here is a pretty cotton chintz with a painterly floral pattern of wild flowers in

yellow, blue, and pink. Choose a fabric that can be easily washed.

These chairs have been decorated very simply because anything ornate would look out of place in most gardens. However, if you wanted to adapt this idea for indoor dining chairs you could use a heavier fabric, such as a cotton damask or jacquard, and trim it with cord piping, tassels, or fringing.

YOU WILL NEED

MAIN FABRIC
LINING FABRIC
MATCHING SEWING THREAD
MEDIUM-WEIGHT BATTING

MEASURING

Measure the width and depth of the seat, back, and base as well as the height of the chair; use these to draw up a pattern for a center piece and a side piece, allowing an extra ¾in (2cm) each way for ease, and adding ¾in (2cm) for each seam allowance. (The seams will be trimmed, but this gives you an extra safety margin.)

1 Use your pattern to cut out one center piece and two side pieces from the main fabric. Cut the same from the lining, but allow fractionally less for ease. Cut out a piece of batting for the seat and inner back only.

2 Lay the center lining piece on the chair, wrong side up. Place the batting on top over the seat and inner back. Baste to the lining. Baste the inner back to the outer back on each side, creating round corners at the top.

3 With right sides together, pin and baste each side piece to the seat at the top and front edges. Also pin and baste each side piece to the outer back for about 7in (18cm), leaving it open beneath that. Remove the lining from the chair and stitch all the seams. Trim the seams and corners, remove the basting, and press.

4 Make up the main fabric cover in the same way as for the lining, but before basting it, put the lining back on the chair, and slip the pinned fabric cover over it to check for fit. Adjust the pins if necessary, and then baste, stitch, and finish as before.

5 Place the lining on the chair again, wrong side out, and slip the fabric cover over it, right side up. Baste the cover and lining together along the seamlines. On the lining, turn ¼in (5mm) and then ½in (1.5cm) to the wrong side along the hem and the open side seams. On the fabric cover, turn the same amount to the wrong side. Topstitch the hem and along the open sides, stitching through both the main fabric and the lining. Remove the cover from the chair, and hand sew or machine stitch the main fabric to the lining along the seamlines.

CANOPIED DECKCHAIR

YOU WILL NEED

DECKCHAIR WITH CANOPY FRAME
THICK COTTON FABRIC SUCH AS TICKING,
CANVAS, OR UPHOLSTERY FABRIC
STRONG MATCHING THREAD
STIFF INTERFACING
UPHOLSTERY TACKS

What could be more relaxing than stretching out on an old-fashioned deckchair, with your head shaded from the sun and your feet comfortably supported?

This deckchair is an old one that has been re-covered in a thick cotton ticking. It is important to choose a sturdy fabric because it must not only support your weight, or that of a guest, but must also withstand the effects that the sun and rain can have on it. The scalloped canopy does not have to be sturdy, but its interior will be clearly visible so you should either line it (as here) or finish off the hems and seams neatly.

1 Remove the cover and measure it. Cut one length of fabric to twice the width of the cover plus ¾in (2cm) for a seam allowance, by the length plus 1½in (4cm).

2 Fold the fabric in half lengthwise, with right sides together, and stitch down the side leaving an opening for turning right side out later. Refold so that the seam runs down the middle, then stitch across both ends. Trim the corners, turn right side out, and slip-stitch the opening to close. Press.

3 Lay the cover wrong side up, then up-end the chair frame over it. Wrap the fabric around the dowels of the chair and hammer in upholstery tacks along the length of each dowel.

4 For the lined canopy, remove the old canopy and measure it. Cut two fabric pieces for the roof, adding ½in (1.25cm) all around. Cut out two fabric strips to wrap around all four sides for the valance. Make the valance in the same way as for the interfaced, lined valance of the tent (page 127, steps 3 and 4), but cut scallops on three sides, leaving the back side straight, and

taking only a ½in (1.25cm) seam allowance. Topstitch along the lower edge if desired. Join the ends.

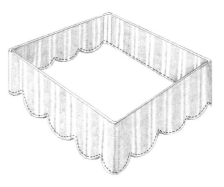

5 Stitch the valance to the outer roof piece with right sides together, clipping into the seam allowance of the valance at the corners as for the tent (page 127, step 2).

6 Turn under ½in (1.25cm) on all four edges of the lining, and hand sew the lining to the wrong side of the canopy roof. Press. Lay the canopy over the canopy frame and secure it at the top with upholstery tacks.

DECORATED ICE BOWL

YOU WILL NEED

2 BOWLS, ONE 1IN (2.5CM) LARGER THAN
THE OTHER
ROSE PETALS AND OTHER EDIBLE FLOWERS
HERBS

One of the most attractive ways of serving summer fruits or ice cream is in a flowery ice bowl. It is easy to make and glorious to look at but, once out of the freezer, its life span is limited.

To make an ice bowl like this, you need two bowls, one larger than the other. The larger one will be the same size as the finished ice bowl so choose your bowl accordingly. Select some rose petals, flowers, and a few sprigs of herbs, then wash them thoroughly but gently. Because the flowers and herbs will be in contact with the food in the ice bowl it is essential to choose plants that are neither poisonous nor have been sprayed with insecticides. Among the flowers suitable for this treatment are nasturtiums, roses, borage, pansies, and dandelions.

1 Pour some cold water into the larger of the two bowls and float the flowers and herbs in it, then gently place the smaller bowl in the larger bowl with a gap of about 1in (2.5cm) between them. Excess water will spill out of the gap between the bowls, so be sure to do this in the sink.

2 When the water has stopped running out, dry the exposed surface of the bowls, and carefully tape them together at intervals around the rim. Transfer them to the freezer and leave until the ice is completely solid.

3 Remove from the freezer about one hour before you will be using the ice bowl, take off the sticky tape, and separate the two bowls. This may be

easier if you quickly dunk the bowls in hot water before separating them.

4 When you have released the ice bowl, replace it in the freezer until you need it. It will quickly start to melt if the weather is hot, so you may wish to place it on an attractive lipped plate to prevent the melting ice from ruining the surface of your table.

LAURA ASHLEY SHOPS

UNITED KINGDOM

LONDON SHOPS
Brent Cross 0181 202 2679
Covent Garden 0171 240 1997
Ealing 0181 579 5197
Kensington 0171 938 3751
Knightsbridge (clothes only)
  0171 823 9700
Knightsbridge (home furnishings only)
  0171 235 9797
Marble Arch 0171 355 1363
Oxford Circus 0171 437 9760

COUNTRY SHOPS
Aberdeen 01224 625787
Aylesbury 01296 84574
Banbury 01295 271295
Barnet 0181 449 9866
Bath 01225 460341
Bedford 01234 211416
Belfast 01232 233313
Beverley 01482 872444
Birmingham 0121 631 2842
Bishops Stortford 01279 655613
Bournemouth (clothes only)
  01202 293764
Brighton 01273 205304
Bristol, Broadmead 0117 922 1011
Bristol, Clifton 0117 927 7468
Bromley 0181 290 6620
Bury St Edmunds 01284 755658
Cambridge 01223 351378
Canterbury 01227 450961
Cardiff 01222 340808
Carlisle 01228 48810
Chelmsford 01245 359602
Cheltenham 01242 580770
Chester (clothes only) 01244 313964
Chester (home furnishings only)
  01244 316403
Chichester 01243 775255
Colchester 01206 562692
Derby 01332 361642
Dudley 01384 79730
Eastbourne 01323 411955
Edinburgh (clothes only) 0131 225 1218
Edinburgh (home furnishings only)
  0131 225 1121
Epsom 01372 739595
Exeter 01392 53949

Farnham 01252 712812
Gateshead 0191 493 2411
Glasgow 0141 226 5040
Guildford 01483 34152
Harrogate 01423 526799
Hereford 01432 272446
High Wycombe 01494 442394
Hitchin 01462 420445
Horsham 01403 259052
Ipswich 01473 216828
Isle of Man 01624 801213
Jersey 01534 608084
Kings Lynn 01553 768881
Kingston 0181 549 0055
Leamington Spa 01926 314584
Leeds 0113 245 0622
Leicester 01162 513165
Lincoln 01522 511611
Llanidloes 01686 412557
Maidstone 01622 750138
Manchester 0161 834 7335
Middlesbrough 01642 226034
Milton Keynes 01908 660190
Newcastle-Under-Lyme 01782 662014
Newport I.O.W. 01983 821806
Northampton (clothes only)
  01604 231975
Norwich 01603 632958
Nottingham 01159 503366
Oxford 01865 791689
Perth 01738 623141
Peterborough 01733 311766
Plymouth 01752 268344
Preston 01772 202425
Reading 01734 594313
Richmond 0181 940 9556
Salisbury 01722 338383
Sheffield 0114 270 1855
Sheffield Meadowhall 0114 256 8221
Shrewsbury 01743 351467
Skipton 01756 700301
Solihull 0121 704 4344
Southampton 01703 228944
Southport 01704 546214
St Albans 01727 864611
Stockport 0161 474 7927
Stratford-Upon-Avon 01789 298852
Sutton 0181 643 9790
Sutton Coldfield 0121 355 3671
Swindon 01793 641727

Taunton 01823 288202
Tenterden 01580 765188
Torquay 01803 291443
Truro 01872 223019
Tunbridge Wells 01892 534431
Watford 01923 254411
Wilmslow 01625 535331
Winchester 01962 855716
Windsor (clothes only) 01753 854345
Windsor (home furnishings only)
  01753 831456
Worcester 01905 20177
Worthing 01903 205160
Yeovil 01935 79863
York 01904 627707

HOMEBASES
Within Sainsbury's Homebase House
  and Garden Centres
Basildon 01268 584088
Basingstoke 01256 469510
Bath 01225 339293
Blackheath 0181 856 9767
Bradford 01274 611929
Branksome 01202 768311
Brentford 0181 847 2214
Camberley 01276 686227
Cardiff 01222 499675
Catford 0181 461 0606
Chichester 01243 533373
Colchester 01206 869187
Coventry 01203 715901
Crawley 01293 538351
Crayford 01322 558614
Croydon 0181 684 8250
Derby 01332 291260
Enfield 0181 366 2236
Falkirk 01324 631551
Gloucester 01452 526806
Guildford 01483 304115
Harlow 01279 413355
Hatfield 01707 275837
Hedge End 01489 789797
Hull 01482 572434
Ilford 0181 590 0212
Ipswich 01473 721124
Kensington 0171 603 2285
Kingston 0181 949 7861
Leeds 0113 268 5010
Leicester 0116 254 6075

Luton 0582 593445
Maidstone 01622 715400
Milton Keynes 01908 692727
New Southgate 0181 368 1698
Newcastle-Under-Lyme 01782 711752
Northampton 01604 234143
Norwich 01603 417474
Nottingham 0115 941 3885
Oldbury 0121 544 7333
Orpington 01689 890353
Oxford 01865 747979
Penge 0181 778 4214
Rayleigh Weir 01268 745374
Reading 01734 584572
Richmond 0181 876 2235
Rochester 01634 200088
Romford 01708 730326
Ruislip 0181 841 8858
Sheffield 0174 255 5175
Stockport 0161 474 7489
Swansea 01792 650935
Swindon 01793 487125
Tunbridge Wells 01892 546646
Wakefield 01924 387011
Waltham Cross 01992 625275
Walthamstow 0181 531 8233
Watford 01923 252075
Wimbledon 0181 946 9802
Worcester 01905 420401
Worle 01934 512628
York 01904 643911

REPUBLIC OF IRELAND
Cork 00 3532 127 4070
Dublin 00 3531 679 5433

UNITED STATES OF AMERICA
Albany 518 452 4998
Ann Arbor 313 747 6620
Ardmore 610 896 0208
Arlington 703 415 2111
Atlanta-Lenox 404 231 0685
Atlanta-Perimeter 770 395 6027
Austin 512 451 4036
Bal Harbor 305 864 5628
Beachwood 216 831 7621
Birch Run 517 624 9297
Birmingham 205 985 0090
Bluffton 803 837 2366
Boca Raton 407 368 5622
Boston 617 536 0505
Bridgewater 908 725 3700
Buffalo 716 681 8600
Burlington MA 617 272 4540

Burlington VT 802 658 5006
Carmel-by-the-Sea 408 624 8095
Central Valley 914 928 4561
Charleston 803 723 3967
Charlotte 704 362 0926
Charlottesville 804 971 7707
Chattanooga 615 855 5496
Chestnut Hill 617 965 7640
Chicago 312 951 8004
Cincinnati 513 793 5535
Columbus 614 224 5057
Corte Madera 415 924 5770
Costa Mesa 714 545 9322
Cranston 401 946 1211
Dallas-Galleria 214 980 9858
Danbury 203 790 5068
Dayton 513 299 9007
Denver-Cherry Creek 303 322 9401
Des Moines 515 243 8881
Destin 904 654 2626
Edina 612 920 2811
Fairfax 703 352 7960
Farmington 203 521 8967
Fort Lauderdale 305 563 2300
Fort Worth 817 346 4666
Freeport 207 865 3300
Germantown 901 756 7036
Gilroy 408 848 5470
Glendale 818 242 0428
Grand Rapids 616 942 6828
Greenville 302 575 1653
Greenwich 203 661 5678
Grosse Pointe 313 886 6960
Hackensack 201 488 0130
Hingham 617 740 4122
Honolulu 808 942 5200
Houston 713 871 9669
Houston/West Oaks 713 558 6113
Indianapolis 317 848 9855
Jacksonville 904 358 7548
Jeffersonville 614 948 2016
Kansas City 816 931 0731
King of Prussia 610 354 9137
Knoxville 615 558 6385
Lake Forest 708 615 1405
Lancaster 717 397 7116
Lexington 606 253 1724
Little Rock 501 666 0272
Los Angeles 310 553 0807
Louisville 502 585 2424
Manhasset 516 365 4834
McLean 703 827 0074
Miami 305 233 8911
Milwaukee 114 347 1930

Minnetonka 612 546 4613
Montgomery 205 284 7011
Myrtle Beach 803 236 4244
Nashville 615 383 0131
New Haven 203 782 9436
New Orleans 504 522 9403
New York City/Westside 212 496 5110
North Bethesda 301 984 3223
Northbrook 708 480 1660
Novi 313 348 9260
Oakbrook 708 572 9195
Oklahoma City 405 848 6252
Omaha 402 390 2085
Orlando 407 351 2785
Osage Beach 314 348 1333
Owings Mills 410 363 2455
Palm Beach 407 832 3188
Palm Beach Gardens 407 624 5901
Palm Springs 619 322 2099
Palo Alto 415 328 0560
Phoenix 602 956 6043
Pittsburgh 412 367 8881
Pittsburgh 412 621 0735
Pleasanton 510 463 8714
Portland 503 224 0703
Prince William 703 474 3124
Princeton 609 683 4760
Raleigh 919 781 1076
Reading 215 373 5495
Redondo Beach 310 542 4436
Richmond 804 740 1406
Ridgeland 601 957 9063
Rochester 507 287 1073
Sacramento 916 923 5696
Salt Lake City 801 363 8408
San Antonio 512 377 2833
San Diego 619 234 0663
San Diego 619 452 6116
San Francisco 415 788 0190
San Marcos 512 396 5570
Santa Ana 714 834 1211
Santa Barbara 805 682 8878
Santa Clara 408 244 3551
Scarsdale 914 723 8500
Schaumberg 708 619 9110
Seattle 206 343 9637
Secausus 201 863 3066
Short Hills 201 467 5657
Skokie 708 673 6604
Southampton 516 287 2104
Stamford 203 324 1067
Stony Brook 516 689 6622
St Augustine 904 823 9533
St Louis 314 993 4410

Tampa 813 253 2177
Towson 410 825 0362
Troy 810 649 0890
Tulsa 918 749 5001
Walnut Creek 510 947 5920
Westport 203 226 7495
White Plains 914 686 3404
Williamsburg 804 229 0353
Winston Salem 919 760 3733
Winter Park 407 740 8900
Woodbury 516 367 2810
Woodland Hills 818 346 7560
Worthington 614 433 9011

MOTHER AND CHILD STORES
Birmingham 205 987 7566
Chestnut Hill 617 965 5687
Denver-Cherry Creek 303 322 9403
Farmington-Hartford 203 561 4870
Hackensack-Riverside 201 342 1222
Houston 713 622 2262
Kansas City 816 931 2810
King of Prussia 610 354 9137
Princeton 609 683 1300
Redondo Beach 310 542 6228
Schaumberg 708 240 1910
Short Hills 201 564 9600
Stamford 203 359 9902
Tulsa 918 749 5001
Walnut Creek 510 947 3932

HOME FURNISHING STORES
Alexandria 701 739 2144
Ardmore 215 896 8293
Atlanta 404 842 0102
Boston 617 357 5151
Burlingame 415 344 1774
Costa Mesa 714 545 7927
Kansas City 816 531 8971
New York City 212 735 5000
Ridgewood 201 670 0868
Short Hills 201 912 9150
Washington 202 686 1200

CANADA
Willowdale 416 223 9507
Calgary, Alberta 403 269 4090
London, Ontario 519 434 1703
Montreal 514 284 9225
Ottawa 613 238 4882
Quebec 418 659 6660
Sherway Gardens, Etobicoke
  416 620 7222
Toronto 416 922 7761

Toronto-Yorkdale 416 256 2040
Vancouver 604 688 8729
Winnipeg 204 943 3093

AUSTRIA
Graz 0316 844398
Innsbruck 0152 579254/579257
Linz 070 797700
Salzburg 0662 840344
Vienna 01 5129312

BELGIUM
Antwerp 03 2343461
Bruges 050 349059
Brussels (clothes only) 02 5112813
Brussels (home furnishings only)
  02 5120447
Gent 092 240819

FRANCE
Paris
94 rue de Rennes 1 45 48 43 89
95 Avenue Raymond Poincaré
  1 45 01 24 73
261 rue Saint Honoré 1 42 86 84 13
Galeries Lafayette, 40 bld Haussmann
  second floor (clothes only)
  1 42 82 34 56
  fifth floor (home furnishings only)
  1 42 82 04 11
Au Printemps, 64 bld Haussmann
  second floor (clothes only)
  1 42 82 52 10
  seventh floor (home furnishings only)
  1 42 82 44 20
Au Printemps, Centre Commercial Vélizy
  Avenue de L'Europe, Vélizy,
  Villacoublay
  Niveau 2 (clothes and home
  furnishings) 1 30 70 87 66
Au Printemps, Centre Commercial
  Parly 2
  Avenue Charles de Gaulle,
  Le Chesnay
  Niveau 1 (home furnishings only)
  1 39 54 22 44 ext. NR 247
  Niveau 2 (clothes only)
  1 39 54 22 44 ext. NR321
Aix-en-Provence 42 27 31 92
Bordeaux 56 44 10 30
Clermont-Ferrand 73 31 22 05
Dijon 80 30 04 44
Lille 20 06 90 06
Lyon 78 37 18 19

Montpellier 67 60 75 75
Nancy 83 35 21 09
Nantes 40 73 17 18
Nice 93 16 06 93
Rouen 35 70 20 02
Strasbourg 88 75 18 90
Toulon 94 21 89 58
Toulouse 61 21 38 85

GERMANY
Augsburg 0821 154021
Berlin (home furnishings only)
  030 8826201
Berlin (clothes only) 030 8824934
Berlin (Kadewe) 030 2183016
Bielefeld 0521 177188
Bonn 0228 654908
Bremen 0421 170443
Cologne 0221 2580470
Dortmund 0231 141009
Düsseldorf 0211 327000
Essen 0201 200482
Frankfurt 069 288791
Hamburg 040 371173
Hanover 0511 326919
Heidelberg 06 22 1189851
Karlsruhe 0721 25968
Munich 089 2608224
Münster 0251 42272
Nürenberg 0911 2451819
Stuttgart 0711 2261064
Wiesbaden 0611 302086

ITALY
Milan 02 86463532

LUXEMBOURG
Luxembourg 221 320

NETHERLANDS
Amsterdam 020 6228087
Arnhem 026 4430250
Eindhoven 040 2435022
Groningen 050 3185060
The Hague 070 3600540
Maastricht 043 3250972
Rotterdam 010 4148535
Utrecht 030 2313051

SPAIN
Barcelona 93 4125490

SWITZERLAND
Basel 061 2619757

Bern 031 3120696
Geneva (clothes only) 022 33113494
Geneva (home furnishings only)
  022 33103048
Zurich 01 2211394

ASIA
HONG KONG SHOPS IN SHOPS
Sogo 852 2891 1767

JAPAN
Ginza 03 3571 5011
Yagoto 052 836 7086
Kichijoji 0422 21 1203
Jiyugaoka 03 3724 0051
Jiyugaoka G (home furnishings only)
  03 5701 5471
Yokohama LMP 045 222 5308
Futako Tamagawa 03 3708 3151
Gifu Melsa 0582 66 3136
Fukuoka Tenjin 092 716 7415
Sapporo Factory 011 207 4031

SHOPS IN SHOPS
TOKYO
Mitsukoshi Nihonbashi 03 3241 5617

Mitsukoshi Ikebukuro 03 3987 6074
Tokyu 03 3477 3836
Keio Shinjuku 03 3344 0080
Mitsukoshi Ginza 03 3561 4050
Tobu Ikebukuro 03 3980 0041

REST OF JAPAN
Mitsukoshi Yokohama 045 323 1683
Saikaya Kawasaki 044 211 8581
Saikaya Yokosuka 046 823 1234
Chiba Mitsukoshi 043 227 4731
Mitsukoshi Bandai 025 243 6333
Sapporo Tokyu 011 212 2658
Kintetsu Abeno 06 625 2332
Hankyu Umeda 06 365 0793
Kawanishi Hankyu 0727 56 1622
Mitsukoshi Hiroshima 082 241 5055
Hiroshima Sogo 082 225 2955
Hakata Izutsuya 092 452 2181
Nagoya Mitsukoshi 052 252 1838
Matsuzakaya Nagoyecki 052 565 4339
Seishin Sogo 078 992 1586
Kobe Ilankyu 078 360 7528
Daimaru Kobe 078 333 4079
Tama Sogo 0423 39 2450
Kintetsu Kyoto 075 365 8024

Be Me Machida Daimaru 0427 24 8174
Sanyo Himeji 0792 23 4792
Tenmaya Fukuyama 0849 27 2214
Mitsukoshi Matsuyama 0899 46 4829
Saikaya Fujisawa 0466 27 1111
Matsuzakaya Yokkaichi 0593 551241
Cita Tokiwa 0975 33 1741
Bon Belta Narita 0476 23 3236
Hamamatsu Matsubishi 053 452 2941
Kagoshima Mitsukoshi 0992 39 4635
Saga Tamaya 0952 28 0608
Kintetsu Nara 0742 30 2751
Kokura Izutsuya 093 522 2627
Kyoto Takashimaya 075 252 7952

SINGAPORE
SHOPS IN SHOPS
Sogo 65 334 1014
Isetan Scotts 65 735 0495

TAIWAN
SHOPS IN SHOPS
Ta-Lee Isetan 886 7 241 8860
Pacific Sogo 886 2 740 9662
Shin Kong Mitsukoshi 886 2 382 4859

ACKNOWLEDGMENTS

The author would like to thank everyone who worked on the project, and also Chelsey Fox and Bill Martin for their behind-the-scenes support.

The publishers would like to thank Mary Batten, Jemima Dyson, Chris Churchley, Denize Lohan, Petra Boase, Linda Bramble, James Ward, Marc Boase, Jim Sugden, and Derek Sutton for their help in the production of this book.

The publishers would also like to thank the following, who kindly loaned props for the photographs: Artisan (0171-498 6974); The Dining Room Shop, 62-64 White Hart Lane, Barnes, London SW13 (0181-878 1020); Global Village, 249 Fulham Road, London SW6; H R W Antiques, 26 Sullivan Road, London SW6; Ian Mankin, Wandsworth Bridge Road, London SW6; Perez Carpets Gallery, 50 Wandsworth Bridge Road, London SW6; Robert Young Antiques, 68 Battersea Bridge Road, London SW11 3AG.

The photographs on pages 3, 7, 8–9, 11, 13, 14, 16, 21 and 80 are from the Laura Ashley Archives. Those on pages 14 and 16 are by Simon Smith. All other photographs are by David Brittain.

INDEX